LIFE IN
THE UNIVERSE

by

FRANCIS JACKSON

M.B., B.S., M.R.C.S., L.R.C.P.,
Dip. Bact. (Lond.), F.R.A.S.

and

PATRICK MOORE

F.R.A.S., F.R.S.A.

W · W · NORTON & COMPANY · INC · *New York*

COPYRIGHT © 1962 BY
FRANCIS JACKSON AND PATRICK MOORE

Library of Congress Catalog Card No. 61-13044

PRINTED IN THE UNITED STATES OF AMERICA

CONTENTS

PLATES

between pages 50-51

FIGURES

PREFACE

Of all the problems facing mankind, that of life in the universe is probably the most fascinating. Are we alone in space?—or do other beings exist, possibly more advanced than ourselves? What is the truth about the canals of Mars—and can men exist on Venus? How many planet-families exist in the Galaxy, and are we likely to find worlds which are similar to the Earth on which we live?

The astronomer is no longer a 'man apart'. His science has joined with mathematics, physics, chemistry and engineering; two of its newest branches, radio astronomy and rocket astronomy, seem likely to increase our knowledge tremendously within the next few years. It is time, then, to bring together astronomy on the one hand, and biology and botany on the other.

The present book is an attempt to examine this whole question, and to summarize the conclusions which may be drawn. Of the two authors, one (Jackson) is a research bacteriologist, while the other (Moore) has for many years carried out observations of the Moon and planets. It is hoped to show that these two disciplines can be usefully combined in a joint approach to the problem of extra-terrestrial life.

It is assumed that the reader has some basic astronomical knowledge, but technical terms used in the text have been defined, and adequate references given. The authors hope that in treating the subject in this way, they have produced some material which will not be without interest.

I

THE UNIVERSE AROUND US

Life on the Earth can take many forms. Man, the most advanced of the mammals, cannot be regarded as physically hardy, but he is able to survive under rigorous conditions by virtue of his superior intelligence; animals of various kinds exist all over the Earth, from the hottest to the coldest; plants are even more adaptable, and primitive micro-organisms are to be found in the most unlikely-sounding places, from hot springs to polar caverns.

Conditions on other worlds are different. The Moon, our nearest neighbour in space, is virtually without atmosphere; Mars is less overwhelmingly hostile, but the atmospheric mantle there is tenuous and oxygen-poor; about Venus we know little, and the remaining planets are clearly unsuitable for advanced life. However, we must remember that our Solar System is only a very small part of the universe, and in discussing the problem of life we must take care not to be parochial. Our first task, then, is to see what the astronomer has to tell us.

Status of the Earth. Originally the Earth was believed to be flat, and to lie in the centre of the universe, with the celestial sphere revolving round it once a day. The earliest astronomers, such as the Chinese and the Egyptians, carried out accurate positional observations of the various bodies in the sky, but made surprisingly little effort to explain them; and it was only with the advent of the Greek philosophers that astronomy became a true science. The first of the philosophers of the Ionian school was Thales of Miletus, who flourished around 600 B.C.; the last great astronomer of Classical times, Ptolemy (Claudius Ptolemæus), died about A.D. 180. During the intervening seven centuries, human knowledge increased enormously.

Thales seems to have learned much of his basic astronomy

1

from the Egyptians, and his ideas were naturally primitive. His younger contemporary, Anaximander, held that the Sun was equal in size to the Earth—in contrast to Heraclitus of Ephesus, who was born about 544 B.C., and who maintained that the solar diameter was about twelve inches. However, the first great step forward was the discovery that the Earth is not flat, but spherical. Pythagoras of Samos, born about 572 B.C., may well have been the first to maintain that the Earth is a globe.

Even in the greatest days of Greece, prejudice was far from absent. One sufferer from it was Anaxagoras of Clazomenæ, who was born about 500 B.C., and enjoyed the friendship and protection of Pericles. Anaxagoras maintained that the Sun was a red-hot stone larger than the Peloponnesus, and the Moon 'earthy'. For these views he was accused of impiety, and was banished from Athens.

The second great step was taken by Aristarchus of Samos (310–230 B.C.). By his day, the spherical nature of the Earth was taken for granted, but it was also assumed that our world must be the centre of the universe, with the Sun, Moon, planets and stars circling round it. Aristarchus boldly dethroned the Earth from this proud position, and put forward the heliocentric theory, according to which the Earth moves round the Sun. Unfortunately he found few followers, and later Greek philosophers returned to the old, erroneous idea. Indeed, it was not until the seventeenth century that the geocentric hypothesis was finally discarded.

The Scale of the Universe. But even though the Greeks, in general, believed the Earth to be the supreme body of the heavens, they formed a reasonably good idea of the scale of the universe. Aristarchus himself wrote a treatise entitled *On the Sizes and Distances of the Sun and Moon*; Eratosthenes of Cyrene, librarian at Alexandria, measured the circumference of the Earth with remarkable accuracy; and the last of the great astronomers of the Greek school, Hipparchus and Ptolemy, left astronomy in a flourishing state. It was known that the universe was of great extent, and that the Moon and planets were worlds in their own right, while the stars were extremely remote and—presumably—self-luminous. Mention must also be made of

Plutarch, who wrote a curious and apparently incomplete essay entitled *De Facie in Orbe Lunæ*. The scientific ideas in this treatise were probably not Plutarch's own, but he did state that the Moon is 'cleft with many deep caves and ruptures', and gave his view that to suppose life to exist on the Moon was no more incredible than assuming life to exist in the terrestrial oceans.

This is a significant statement. To Plutarch, the Moon was an 'earthy' world; he could not know that it lacks atmosphere, and there seemed no obvious reason to doubt its habitability. Why should not life appear wherever conditions were suitable for it?

Ancient astronomy ends abruptly with the death of Ptolemy, whose great book, known to us by its Arab title of the *Almagest*, provides us with an excellent summary of the scientific knowledge which had been accumulated in Classical times. A long period of stagnation followed, and then progress began once more. Excellent positional observations were made by the Arabs, and the new learning spread over Europe. In 1546 came the publication of the immortal *De Revolutionibus Orbium Cœlestium* of Nicolaus Copernicus, which cast aside the Ptolemaic theory of the universe and replaced the Sun in the centre of the Solar System; later in the sixteenth century Tycho Brahe, of Denmark, made precise observations of the positions of the stars and the movements of the planets, thereby enabling his assistant and successor, Johannes Kepler, to establish the heliocentric theory once and for all; in 1608 the telescope was invented, and during the winter of 1609–10 Galileo first applied it to the heavens. Before the end of the seventeenth century, the work of Sir Isaac Newton had ushered in the new era.

In 1600, the science of astronomy was in a more or less mediæval condition, mainly because it was limited to naked-eye studies. The size of the Earth was by no means certainly known (Columbus, on his voyage of discovery, used a value which was less accurate than that of Eratosthenes), and the official view was still that the Sun moved round the Earth. By 1700, all was changed. The geocentric hypothesis had gone forever, and the outlook had become essentially modern. Ole Rømer had determined the velocity of light with considerable accuracy, and it was known that the distance of the Sun was something like 90,000,000 miles, which enabled astronomers to determine the scale of the Solar System adequately. The Earth had been relegated to the status of a normal planet, much inferior in size to some of its companions such as Jupiter and Saturn.

Star Distances. Another outstanding problem, that of the distances of the stars, proved to be difficult to solve. Success came finally in 1838, when Bessel, at Königsberg, used the parallax method to show that a fifth-magnitude star in the constellation of the Swan, 61 Cygni, is roughly 11 light-years away from us. One light-year, the distance traversed by a ray of light in one year, is equal to about 5,880,000,000,000 (nearly 6 million million) miles, and so 61 Cygni is indeed remote; even so, only a few closer stars have been found. Pride of place goes to a faint red dwarf in the southern hemisphere, Proxima Centauri, whose distance is 4·3 light-years.

As soon as some star-distances became known, the luminosities of the stars concerned could be worked out, and it became clear that the Sun is by no means distinguished. Sirius, which shines as the brightest star in the sky, is 8·6 light-years away, and is 26 times more luminous than the Sun; Rigel in Orion, with a distance of over 500 light-years, is equal to at least 18,000 Suns; the most luminous stars known to us are at least a million times brighter than the Sun. On the other hand, we must not become too humble. Just as the stellar system includes 'searchlights', so it also includes 'glow-worms', and many of the dwarf stars are far inferior to the Sun in real luminosity.

For our present purpose, the most interesting question is whether any of these stars may be the centres of planetary systems. This problem will be discussed in more detail in Chapter VIII, but meanwhile it is worth noting that there seem to be many stars in the Galaxy which are remarkably similar to the Sun. When we remember that our Galaxy is only one of millions, the chances that other planetary systems exist appear to be overwhelmingly great.

Bodies of the Solar System. The Solar System consists of one star (the Sun), nine planets, and various lesser bodies such as satellites, comets, asteroids and meteors. The Sun itself has a diameter of 864,000 miles, and a surface temperature of 6000° C.; at its centre the temperature must rise to around 15,000,000° C., and it is here that energy is being produced by nuclear reactions. The Sun is a typical *Main Sequence* star, and its life expectation must be reckoned in thousands of millions of years.

The planets are divided into two main groups. The inner group consists of four comparatively small worlds—Mercury, Venus, the Earth and Mars. Mercury is not a great deal larger than the Moon, and is almost devoid of atmosphere; moreover its *sidereal period* (time taken to revolve once round the Sun) coincides with its axial rotation period, so that part of the surface is permanently sunlit and another part permanently dark. Venus is about the same size as the Earth, but its actual surface is never visible to us, since it is masked by a considerable atmosphere containing a great deal of carbon dioxide, together with water-vapour. Mars, the first planet beyond the orbit of the Earth, has a diameter of 4200 miles, and has a thin atmosphere which is very poor in oxygen and water-vapour.

Beyond Mars comes a region containing thousands of dwarf worlds known as the minor planets or *asteroids*. Ceres, the largest of them, is less than 500 miles in diameter, and all must be dismissed as airless lumps of material. Probably many of the smaller asteroids are not even approximately spherical.

Further out we come to the giants, Jupiter, Saturn, Uranus and Neptune. These worlds are very different in nature from the inner planets, and their surfaces are not solid. They seem to be composed of gas (largely hydrogen), and their temperatures are extremely low. Finally we come to Pluto, which is about the size of Mars, and has a mean distance from the Sun of well over 3,000,000,000 miles.

The satellites, secondary bodies accompanying some of the planets, are of interest in our present theme. The Earth has of course one satellite only; the Moon, which is 239,000 miles away, and has a diameter of 2160 miles. It is worth noting that the nearest planet, Venus, is always at least 100 times as remote as the Moon, while Mars is more distant still, and never comes much within 35,000,000 miles of us. Even our greatest telescopes will not give a better view of Mars than may be obtained of the

Moon with good binoculars, and it is no wonder that our knowledge remains incomplete.

For the moment we need spend no time in discussing the junior members of the Solar System, the comets and meteors. It is also pointless to speculate as to the existence of further planets beyond the orbit of Pluto. As a matter of fact, it is quite probable that one or more trans-Plutonian planets exist, and searches are made for them from time to time; but in any case they must be very faint, and will be bitterly cold.

So far as Earth-type life is concerned, the only planets in the Solar System which appear to hold out any hopes are Venus and Mars. Yet so far we have confined ourselves to relatively close bodies—even Pluto, on the fringe of the Sun's kingdom, must be regarded as a near neighbour of ours according to the distance-scale of the universe—so let us look further afield.

The Stellar Universe. The star-system or Galaxy in which the Sun is situated contains perhaps 100,000 million stars, ranging from very luminous supergiants through solar-type stars down to dim red dwarfs. The Galaxy takes the form of a flattened disk with a central nucleus, and is about 100,000 light-years from side to side; its greatest 'thickness' is estimated at 20,000 light-years. The Sun is not centrally situated, but lies well out toward one edge, and is thought to be between 25,000 and 30,000 light-years from the galactic centre.

The general form of the Galaxy was first determined by Sir William Herschel, who is popularly remembered for his discovery of the planet Uranus in 1781, but whose chief work was in connection with the stars. Herschel was mistaken in thinking the Sun to lie near the centre of the system, but his basic concept has proved to be correct. Herschel also found that many of the stars are members of *binary* systems, consisting of two (or more) stars which are physically associated and in common revolution; in addition, he catalogued many of the objects known as *nebulæ*, which are very common in the Galaxy.

Herschel's 'nebulæ' were of two main kinds. One type appeared to be non-stellar; the best example is Messier 42, in the Sword of Orion, not far from the three bright stars which make up the Hunter's Belt. Other objects, such as Messier 31 in Andromeda, showed indications of resolution into stars. Herschel made the brilliant speculation that these resolvable objects might be separate stellar systems, far beyond the boundary of our own Galaxy.

When Herschel died, in 1822, stellar distances were unknown. Even when the parallax method was successfully applied by Bessel and others, the distances of the resolvable nebulæ remained a problem; they showed no measurable parallaxes, and so were obviously remote. The question was finally cleared up, in our own century, by an indirect method.

Most stars, including the Sun, shine steadily over very long periods. Others show short-term fluctuations of light, and are known as *variables*. Among these variables are the Cepheids, so called because the brightest member of the class is Delta in the constellation of Cepheus. It was found that the real luminosity of a Cepheid is linked with its period of fluctuation—the longer the period, or time taken to pass from maximum to maximum, the more luminous the Cepheid. It thus became possible to determine the distances of the Cepheids merely by observing their changes in light.

In 1923 Hubble, using the 100-inch Hooker reflector at Mount Wilson, detected Cepheids in Messier 31, the famous 'resolvable nebula' in Andromeda. He was able to make an estimate of the distances of the Cepheids, and hence of the system in which they lay. At once the problem was solved: Messier 31 lay at an immense distance, and was a separate system—a galaxy in its own right. Modern measures place it at a distance of about 2,000,000 light-years. We also know that Messier 31 is a system larger than our own, and it too includes features such as star-clusters and gaseous nebulæ. It is spiral in form; during the last decade, radio astronomy has proved that our Galaxy also is spiral.

Once the basic problem had been dealt with, astronomers were able to draw up a much more accurate picture of the universe. The 200-inch Palomar reflector is capable of showing about 1000 million galaxies, some of them so remote that they appear as nothing more than fuzzy specks upon long-exposure photographic plates. The most distant galaxy so far measured lies at a distance of about 5000 million light-years. Not all the

7

systems are spiral (in fact, spirals appear to be in the minority), but each contains a host of stars of all kinds. Spectroscopic studies indicate that apart from members of our local group of galaxies, of which Messier 31 is one, all these systems are receding at high speeds, so that the whole universe is expanding. The greatest recessional velocity so far measured is almost 90,000 miles per second. Of course, many more galaxies must exist beyond the observable range of the Palomar reflector, and the completion of the new 236-inch telescope now under construction in Russia will be eagerly awaited.

Let us re-examine the whole situation in the light of this new concept of the universe, and see how it affects our ideas as to the frequency of life.

The Sun, a normal star, controls a planetary system consisting of nine known members. One of these is the Earth; two more, Venus and Mars, are sufficiently earth-like to be considered as possible abodes of life, even if of lowly form. The Galaxy contains 100,000 million stars, many of which are solar in type. The observable universe includes 1000 million galaxies, and if we accept our own system as being of average size (which is very probable) the number of suns which we know to exist works out at 100,000 million multiplied by 1000 million. Under the circumstances, it is surely the height of conceit to suppose that our Sun is unique in being attended by an inhabited planet. Our ideas have changed drastically indeed since the days when men thought the Earth to lie at the centre of the universe, and to be the most important body in the heavens.

So much for the astronomer's viewpoint. Now let us turn from the almost inconceivably great to the almost inconceivably small, and pay some attention to the structure of living and non-living matter.

The Materials of the Universe. As is well known, the materials we find around us in the world are built up from minute atoms. Substances which consist of one kind of atom are called *elements*, and although atoms of one element cannot be changed into those of another by chemical reactions, transformations have been achieved by physical methods. Radioactive elements consist of unstable atoms, and, as will be described later, these change

8

spontaneously. Atoms of the same, or different, elements frequently unite to form *molecules*, and substances whose molecules contain atoms of two or more different elements are called *compounds*. There are 92 naturally-occurring elements, and in recent years ten more have been produced artificially by physical methods.

An atom may be pictured, in a much over-simplified form, as consisting of a central *nucleus* bearing a positive electric charge, with negatively-charged *electrons* revolving in orbits around it. The positively-charged particles in the nucleus are called *protons*, and each proton weighs about 1850 times as much as an electron. In a complete atom, the number of orbiting electrons is the same as the number of protons in the nucleus, so that the sum of the positive and negative charges is zero and the atom is electrically neutral. The simplest atom, that of hydrogen, consists of a single proton and one electron (Fig. 1a), but the nuclei

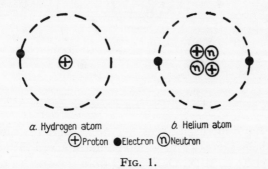

a. Hydrogen atom   *b.* Helium atom

⊕Proton   ●Electron   ⓝNeutron

FIG. 1.

of all other atoms contain, in addition to protons, a number of uncharged particles, *neutrons*. There are at least as many neutrons as protons, usually more, in all atoms other than those of hydrogen; these neutrons are necessary for stability of the nuclei. If an atom loses one or more electrons, it becomes positively charged, because there is then an excess of protons; conversely, an atom which gains one or more electrons will be negatively charged. These charged atoms are termed *ions*.

Hydrogen is the most abundant element, accounting for approximately 93 per cent of the total number of atoms in the universe and 76 per cent of the total weight. The next most common element is helium, about 7 per cent by number of atoms and 23 per cent by weight. All the other elements together constitute only about 1 per cent of the total mass of the universe. The helium atom contains two protons and two neutrons in its nucleus, and therefore has two orbiting electrons (Fig. 1*b*).

The atom of oxygen is more complicated, the nucleus containing eight protons and eight neutrons, so that eight electrons are required for electrical neutrality; these are arranged round the nucleus in two *shells*, an inner shell with two electrons and an outer shell with six (Fig. 2). Elements with larger atoms

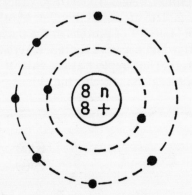

FIG. 2. The Oxygen atom.

naturally have more electrons per atom, and the number of electron shells increases to a maximum of seven. These shells are labelled K, L, M, N, O, P and Q from the nucleus outward. Electrons are not distributed round a nucleus in a haphazard manner. Certain configurations are possible, and of these some are more stable than others. There is an orderliness about atoms; only certain types are possible, and the chemical reactions in which they participate are a result of the details of atomic structure.

The outermost electrons of atoms are the ones mainly concerned in chemical reactions. The capacity of the different shells for electrons is not the same, and the greater the radius of a shell, the more electrons it can contain. If the K, L, M, N . . . shells are numbered 1, 2, 3, 4 . . . and so on, respectively, the maximum number of electrons a shell can accommodate is given by the expression $2n^2$, where n is the number assigned to the shell (the *principal quantum number*). Thus, the K shell can accommodate at most $2 \times 1^2 = 2$ electrons, the L shell $2 \times 2^2 = 8$ electrons, the M shell $2 \times 3^2 = 18$ electrons and the N shell $2 \times 4^2 = 32$ electrons.

We can imagine the series of increasingly complex atoms being built up in an orderly fashion from the necessary 'bricks', protons, electrons and neutrons, the electrons being arranged in the appropriate shells. Hydrogen has one electron in the K shell, and helium two. No more than two electrons can enter the K shell, and so the next element, lithium, with three electrons, has two in the K shell and one in the L shell. With two exceptions, the outermost shell of the atom of an element does not contain more than eight electrons. In the series of elements, when a shell is occupied by eight electrons, no more can be added until the next shell out from the nucleus has been occupied. An atom with a complete 'octet' of eight electrons in the outermost shell is chemically inert, because of the inability of the stable outer octet of electrons to interact with the outermost electron shells of other atoms. The inert gases, neon, argon, krypton and xenon have complete octets in the L, M, N and O shells respectively. Helium is also inert, because its K shell, which can accommodate no more than two electrons, is already full.

The oxygen atom is taken as a basis for the comparison of weights of the atoms of different elements, and is assigned a weight of 16 units. On this scale the weight of the hydrogen atom is 1·008 and the helium atom 4·003. The values arrived at by these comparisons are termed *atomic weights* of the elements; because electrons are so much less massive than protons and neutrons, the atomic weight is determined mainly by the structure of the nucleus. The number of protons, that is to say positive charges, in the nucleus is called the *atomic number*. From the chemical standpoint, atomic number is more important than atomic weight, for it is a direct indication of the number of electrons which the complete, electrically neutral atom possesses.

Development of Atomic Theory. Greek philosophy contained the germs of atomic theory, but it was quite unsupported by evidence, and the modern theory stems mainly from the work of the English chemist John Dalton at the beginning of the nineteenth century. Once the theory was given a sound practical basis, other investigators were naturally anxious to discover more about atoms and their properties. In 1869 the Russian chemist Mendeléyev, elaborating earlier suggestions by Newlands and Döbereiner, proposed a 'periodic table' of elements. He noticed that if a list were made of elements in order of atomic weights, there was a periodic change of properties of the elements in the table. Moreover, it was apparent that the table which could be constructed at that time was incomplete, and Mendeléyev was able to forecast, with remarkable accuracy, the main properties of some elements which had not then been discovered.

Later work extended and modified Mendeléyev's periodic table, and it is now clear that the regularities noticed by the great Russian chemist have a sound basis in atomic structure. The recognition that the chemical properties of elements are more closely related to atomic number than to atomic weights has thrown light on some anomalies of early versions of the periodic table.

Isotopes. It was at first thought that all atoms of a given element were identical, but this is not so. Many elements exist in forms which have the same atomic number, but which, because they have different numbers of neutrons in the nuclei, differ in atomic weight. These chemically similar, but physically distinguishable forms of an element are known as *isotopes* (Greek = 'same place'), because they occupy the same place in the periodic table. The ordinary hydrogen atom consists of a single proton and electron, but there are atoms which consist of one proton, one neutron and one electron (deuterium), and one proton, two neutrons and one electron (tritium). Deuterium and tritium are, therefore, isotopes of hydrogen. The deuterium atom is stable, but the tritium nucleus disintegrates spontaneously with the emission of radiation, and so is *radioactive* (see below). Hydrogen, deuterium and tritium have similar chemical properties, but the atom of hydrogen itself, because of its small dimensions, is in some ways a special case.

We will see later that the differences in the ability of the isotopes of hydrogen to form what are termed *hydrogen bonds* with certain other atoms may affect their behaviour when incorporated in large molecules, and render them unsuitable as substitutes for hydrogen in 'biological' molecules. Many other elements have isotopes, both radioactive and non-radioactive, and some isotopes have wide applications in industry, medicine and biological research.

Packing Factor. When protons and neutrons are packed together in an atomic nucleus, the mass of the complete nucleus is found to be less than would be expected if it were a simple sum of the individual masses of the particles involved. The packing or binding of nuclear particles is associated with some loss of mass, and this corresponds to the binding energy which is emitted when nuclei are formed. Physical measurements permit the determination of this loss, or *packing factor*, with a high degree of precision. Einstein's special theory of relativity provides a method for calculating what the mass loss represents in terms of energy. The relationship between mass and energy is expressed in the equation $E = mc^2$, where E is the energy in ergs, m the mass in grammes and c the velocity of light in centimetres per second. The application of this formula reveals that the formation of a gramme of helium from protons and neutrons would be associated with the emission of enough energy to run about 20,000 electric fires of 1000 watts each for 10 hours. The release of energy resulting from the fusion of atomic nuclei forms the basis of thermonuclear, or hydrogen, bombs and may one day, in a saner age, be usefully and constructively employed for the benefit rather than the destruction of man.

Radioactivity. The radiations emitted by radioactive atoms arise from changes in the nuclei. Radium was one of the first radioactive elements investigated, and three different kinds of 'rays', termed by Rutherford alpha-, beta- and gamma-rays, were distinguished. The alpha- and beta-rays were deflected by magnetic fields, and from the direction of deflection it was concluded that alpha-rays were positively charged and beta-rays negatively charged. Later work showed that alpha-rays are streams of particles indistinguishable from the nuclei of helium atoms, while beta-rays are streams of electrons. Gamma-rays are short-wave electromagnetic radiations of the same kind as X-rays and light.

The emission of these radiations is a sign of transformation of one kind of atom into another. The expulsion of an alpha-particle, which in atomic terms has a mass of 4 and a positive charge of 2, lowers the atomic weight by 4 and the atomic number by 2. The emission of a negatively-charged beta-particle, which results from the transformation of a neutron into a proton and an electron, leaves the atom with one more positive charge than it had before. This raises the atomic number by 1—without the atomic weight being appreciably affected, because the weight of the expelled electron is so small compared with that of a proton or a neutron.

In this brief account, only a few aspects of atomic structure have been dealt with, to provide a basis for the understanding of later chapters. Many other particles are known besides protons, electrons and neutrons, and much has yet to be discovered, for instance, about the way in which the nuclear particles of atoms are held together.

There are also 'anti-particles', which correspond to most of the known particles, but have opposite characteristics. The 'anti-proton' is negatively charged, but has the same mass as a proton; the *positron* is, in effect, a positively-charged electron. There is a possibility that whole galaxies may consist of 'anti-matter', built up from anti-protons, positrons and anti-neutrons. Our kind of matter and anti-matter would destroy each other if brought into contact.

Spectroscopy. White light is a mixture of electromagnetic radiations of different wavelengths, and a beam of white light can be split up into its constituent coloured components by means of a spectroscope. The spectrum of visible light extends from violet radiations, with wavelengths of about 4000 Ångström units (1 Ångström unit = 1/10,000,000 of a millimetre) through blue, green, yellow, orange, and finally red light with a wavelength around 7500 Ångström units. Wavelengths shorter than those of violet light form the invisible ultra-violet and X-ray radiations, while radiations of wavelengths longer than red light constitute the invisible infra-red (heat) and radio waves.

An incandescent solid gives a continuous spectrum, in which the colours seen through a spectroscope form a rainbow-like band; but if a glowing gas or vapour is examined spectroscopically, a discontinuous spectrum, consisting of a number of bright lines of light of particular wavelengths, is seen. These lines are emitted by the atoms present in the substance, and their positions are characteristic for each particular element. They are caused by electron jumps within the atoms, and form what is termed an *emission spectrum*.

If an atom absorbs radiant energy, electrons may jump from one orbit to another, further removed from the nucleus. Soon, however, the electrons fall back again to the lower-energy orbit closer to the nucleus, and in this process energy is re-emitted. These jumps are discrete, the electrons passing from one orbit to another without lingering at any intermediate level. If light from a source giving a continuous spectrum is passed through the gas or vapour, then the atoms absorb light of the same wavelength as they would emit under the conditions which have just been described—so that an examination of the light after it has passed through the gas will show deficiencies in the continuous spectrum, which appear as dark lines, in positions characteristic of the elements present. This is termed an *absorption spectrum*.

Spectroscopy can also be applied to the study of molecules, and may give indications of the type of compound present. It is possible to study absorptions in the invisible ultra-violet and infra-red wavebands, so that extra information, not available from the study of visible wavebands alone, may be obtained. There is no space here to describe the methods used, but for our present purpose it is sufficient to say that spectroscopic studies of the planets have yielded information about the atmospheric constitution and, in some cases, surface features. Several examples of this will be described later. For the study of the stars, including our Sun, spectroscopy has provided an enormous amount of information about the elements present, and about stellar temperatures, motions and other related problems. It is not too much to say that the spectroscope is one of the most valuable instruments available to astronomers, physicists, chemists and biologists.

II

THE NATURE AND ORIGIN OF LIVING ORGANISMS ON THE EARTH

Section I : Historical Introduction

The problems of the nature and origin of living things have stimulated speculation and argument for thousands of years, and we can hardly doubt that the apparent differences between living and dead animals and human beings profoundly impressed prehistoric man. First-hand experience of human existence must have been responsible for moulding many of the views of primitive peoples on the nature of life. It was necessary to account not only for the behaviour of active men and animals pursuing their everyday lives, but also for the seemingly mysterious phenomena of sleep, dreams, disease and death. It is probable that dreams about dead persons played an important part in the development of the notion of immortality, and of the belief that the living body is inhabited and rendered alive by a shade or ghost which could, under certain circumstances, lead a separate existence, leaving the body temporarily or permanently. It was frequently thought that the shade, or 'anima' as it has since been termed, might successively inhabit different bodies, animal, human and even plants, a belief also found later in the 'metempsychosis' of the Pythagorian school of Greek philosophers who probably derived it from the Orphic religion. Belief in transmigration of souls was important in ancient Egypt, and is a feature of Buddhism and of the religions of some existing primitive tribes.

To ancient observers, it seemed self-evident that complicated creatures, such as worms and birds, could arise from simpler materials like dirt and earth. Mice appeared to arise from mud and maggots from stale meat. We can distinguish here two sources which were thought capable of generating organisms; first, inorganic materials; and secondly, materials which, although dead, had previously been alive.

The development of organized agriculture and irrigation methods probably influenced thought on the nature of life by broadening man's direct and detailed experience of living things. Crowther[1] has pointed out that the Ionian Greek philosophers, in Asia Minor, probably derived a fairly extensive and objective view of living things from the agricultural Sumerians of Mesopotamia, an outlook less exclusively associated with men and animals than were the earlier ideas of more primitive peoples.

Greek Thought. There was much Greek speculation on the nature and origin of living things, but concerning origins the later Greek philosophers added little of importance to the ideas of the Ionians. Anaximander, a Greek Ionian philosopher who lived in the sixth century B.C., came to the conclusion that living organisms were subject to evolutionary change. He suggested that the motions of a fundamental substance had produced the Sun, planets and stars, that this same substance had given rise to living things which survived by adaptation to their environment, and that man had evolved from a fish-like ancestor. Anaximander believed that the action of the Sun's rays on moist materials had promoted the origin of organisms, and we shall see later that a similar view plays a part in modern theories. These opinions of Anaximander were, when propounded, far in advance of the science of the time, and so could find no substantiation in fact.

Not all philosophers were as far-seeing as Anaximander in their speculations. Oparin[2] quotes the suggestion, attributed to Empedocles (fifth century B.C.) that from the Earth 'many foreheads without necks sprang forth, and arms wandered unattached bereft of shoulders, and eyes strayed about alone needing brows'. Complete bodies, animal and human, he supposed to have been formed by the later union of the individually produced members.

Some early thinkers reached the conclusion that there must be a limit to the divisibility of matter. The development of this theory is particularly associated with Democritus (born about

470 B.C.), who derived the notion from Leucippus (early fifth century B.C.). Living things were supposed to contain a fluid matter of a special kind, made of finer and more mobile ultimate particles, or 'atoms', than those of ordinary solid objects. Much early Greek thought was essentially, if subtly, materialistic, and this is typified by the view that the animating principle was a fine, mobile fluid. The idea of an immaterial spirit or soul was a later development, for the shades envisaged by more primitive peoples had material, if sometimes magical, attributes, and could be appeased by offerings of food and material objects.

Plato (427–347 B.C.) and Aristotle (385–322 B.C.) ascribed the various functions of living bodies to the 'psyche', and distinguished vegetable, animal and intellectual functions. Plato believed that the human psyche was largely independent of the body and capable of a separate existence. Aristotle seems to have regarded the psyche and body ('soma') as inseparable, although he suggested that reasoning might be a manifestation of universal Reason acting through the individual psyche. The works of Plato and Aristotle profoundly influenced the development of Christianity during the next 1500 years, and at the same time the notion of wholly non-material souls grew. It is interesting to note, however, that even some of the Christian fathers did not think of the soul as completely without material qualities, for it was suggested that a non-material soul would not have been able to suffer the torments of Hell, which would have made Hell rather pointless.

We have seen that the belief in spontaneous generation of living things from non-living materials was widespread in the ancient world. Aristotle accepted as fact the spontaneous generation of animals and plants from earth, slime and manure, and his opinions carried great weight for many hundreds of years. It was not until the seventeenth century that careful testing of those beliefs began.[3]

Experimental Approach. The first experiments which gave clear results leading to a questioning of the belief in spontaneous generation were conducted by the Italian, Francesco Redi. In 1668, Redi showed that maggots were not produced on stale meat if the meat were adequately protected from flies, but he continued to believe in some other types of spontaneous generation. A contemporary of Redi was the Dutchman, Anthony van Leeuwenhoek, the first true microbiologist. The methods and findings of this remarkable man have been brilliantly described by Dobell,[4] in his book *Anthony van Leeuwenhoek and his Little Animals*. A master of the art of lens-making, he discovered with his simple microscopes the world of micro-organisms, and reported his findings to the Royal Society, London, in a series of letters. Leeuwenhoek's work led to the recognition of microbes in putrefying materials, and arguments raged about the origin of these tiny creatures. Did they come from the air, or were they generated spontaneously in gravies, soups or other fluids in which they were found?

In the mid-eighteenth century, Spallanzini, another Italian investigator, showed that no microbes appeared in broths subjected to prolonged heating in containers which were quickly sealed before cooling. These findings were challenged by Needham, in England, on the grounds that heating might destroy a 'vegetative force' which resided in the materials used in the experiments. Spallanzini[5] planned and executed a brilliant series of experiments to prove that this was not so. He was able to show, too, that some of the minute creatures which grew and multiplied in soups and broths, were able to carry on their activities after removal of air by means of a vacuum pump. 'How wonderful this is,' he wrote, 'for we have always believed there is no living being that can live without the advantages air offers it.'

The Nineteenth Century. Spallanzini died in 1799, at the beginning of a century of rapid advance in biological knowledge. In 1837, Cagniard de la Tour, a French investigator, found that the fermentation of beer resulted from the activities of tiny organisms. Microscopical examination of fermenting fluids showed that the yeasts present were growing, and multiplying by budding. Schwann, in Germany, demonstrated that putrefaction of meat required the presence of microscopic creatures, and that if these were rigidly excluded meat would remain fresh for long periods of time.

The theory that complicated microbes could be generated in

20

soups and broths in short periods of time received another set-back from the work of the great French scientist, Louis Pasteur.[3] He repeated, with various technical refinements, some of Spallanzini's experiments, and demonstrated that flasks of boiled broths remained sterile unless contaminated by dust from the air. Germs were not developing spontaneously from the broths, but only appeared if unfiltered air could enter the flasks. There was some criticism of Pasteur's results from other investigators, who claimed that heating did not always prevent the appearance of micro-organisms in soups and infusions. Pasteur used boiled yeast broths, but Pouchet and his colleagues tried infusions of hay, which sometimes grew organisms even after heating. The reason for this was discovered later by John Tyndall, in England, who found that hay contains microscopic germs as *spores*, a form which can withstand long periods of boiling in water and require more drastic treatment to kill them.

The work of Spallanzini, Pasteur and Tyndall disposed of the naïve theory of spontaneous generation of microbes, but in no way ruled out the possibility that, in the course of thousands of millions of years living things might have developed from inorganic materials by a long evolutionary process. Tyndall was, as we shall see, an outstanding champion of this view.

Later Developments. During the later part of the nineteenth century and the early twentieth century, discussion of the origin of life led to considerable clarification of the problem. As a result of the writings of Charles Darwin, T. H. Huxley, Tyndall, Schäfer and others, a position was reached which has much in common with present-day views.

Tyndall,[6] in his essay on Vitality (1866), summarized the state of knowledge at that time. He recognized that the energy for life was derived ultimately from the Sun, and that plants were essential for trapping solar energy and played an intermediate rôle in the energy chain from Sun to animals. He emphasized that 'the matter of the animal body is that of inorganic nature. There is no substance in the animal tissues which is not primarily derived from the rocks, the water and the air.' He proceeded to argue that since every portion of an animal body may be reduced to inorganic matter, 'a perfect reversal of this process of reduction would carry us from the inorganic to the organic, and such a reversal is at least conceivable'. Tyndall concluded that it was the special arrangement of elements in living bodies which led to the phenomena of life, and turning to the problem of life's origin he proclaimed, 'In an amorphous drop of water lie latent all the marvels of crystalline force; and who will set limits to the possible play of molecules in a cooling planet?'

It is apparent that this view differs from those earlier theories which postulated a special material principle, of a subtle and tenuous kind, as an essential constituent of living things. The elements of living bodies are not different from those of inorganic nature, but have a special arrangement. In his address to the British Association in Belfast (1874), Tyndall[7] said that he could discern in 'matter which we, in our ignorance of its latent powers, and notwithstanding our professed reverence for its Creator, have previously covered with opprobrium, the promise and potency of all terrestrial life'.

Charles Darwin, who was concerned more particularly with the later evolution of living things, gave some thought to possible processes of life's origin. In a remarkable paragraph, he wrote,[8] 'It is often said that all the conditions for the first production of a living organism are present, which could ever have been present. But if (and Oh! what a big if!) we could conceive in some warm little pond, with all sorts of ammonia and phosphoric salts, light, heat, electricity, etc., present, that a protein compound was chemically formed ready to undergo still more complex changes, at the present day such matter would be instantly devoured or absorbed, which would not have been the case before living creatures were formed.' There are indications that Darwin did not consider the subject one for serious scientific consideration. In a letter to Sir J. Hooker he wrote, 'It is mere rubbish thinking at present of the origin of life; one might as well think of the origin of matter.' Bernal[9] has recently remarked that we are now almost in a position to take Darwin at his word, for the mode of origin of matter in the forms in which we find it on this earth is at last becoming clearer. Bernal warns that we should not accept 'wild hypotheses of the origin of life or of matter—we should attempt almost from the outset to produce careful and logical sequences in which we can hope to demonstrate that certain stages must have preceded certain others, and from these partial sequences gradually build up one coherent story'. This approach is being widely followed at the present time, and already many 'partial sequences', some of them supported by experimental evidence, have been worked out.

We have seen earlier how Tyndall sought to clarify the problem of the nature and origin of living things. At about the same time, Thomas Henry Huxley[10] wrote his discourse *On the Physical Basis of Life*. Like Tyndall, he pointed out that plants can build themselves up from simple materials, whereas animals require more complicated foods. He argued that, in spite of differences in detail, there is a fundamental similarity between living things, 'a single physical basis of life underlying all the diversities of vital existence'. He went on to stress that 'the existence of the matter of life depends on the pre-existence of certain compounds; namely, carbonic acid, water and certain nitrogenous bodies . . . They are as necessary to the protoplasm of the plant as the protoplasm of the plant is to that of the animal. Carbon, hydrogen, oxygen and nitrogen are all lifeless bodies. Of these, carbon and oxygen unite, in certain proportions and under certain conditions, to give rise to carbonic acid: hydrogen and oxygen produce water; nitrogen and other elements give rise to nitrogenous salts. These new compounds, like the elementary bodies of which they are composed, are lifeless. But when they are brought together, under certain conditions, they give rise to the still more complex body, protoplasm, and this protoplasm exhibits the phenomena of life.' Further, he said, 'I see no break in this series of steps in molecular complication, and I am unable to understand why the language which is applicable to any one term of the series may not be used for any of the others.' In the nineteenth century there was still a widespread belief that 'life' was something which worked through, but could be independent of matter. Anyone who questioned this view was exposed to the risk of heavy criticism from religious authorities. Huxley and Tyndall were quite capable of defending themselves when necessary. At least they could no longer be burned at the stake, as was

Giordano Bruno, for expressing unorthodox views, or summoned before priests and subjected to threats and pressures like Galileo. Huxley quoted with approval some words of the philosopher, David Hume: 'If we take in our hand any volume of divinity, or school metaphysics, for instance, let us ask, Does it contain any abstract reasoning concerning quantity or number? No. Does it contain any experimental reasoning concerning matter of fact and existence? No. Commit it then to the flames; for it can contain nothing but sophistry and illusion.'

No further important advances were made until the science of biochemistry began to develop, particularly during the third, fourth and fifth decades of the twentieth century. The problems were clearly formulated during the nineteenth century, but the outlines were broad; there was a lack of chemical and physical knowledge of the functioning of organisms. At the present time, a vast territory still remains to be explored, but the steady advance of biological, chemical and physical research has stimulated a new interest in the origin of life, sharpened by the real possibility of interplanetary travel. The subject is of great complexity, involving many fields of science, and the relevant evidence from various sources should ultimately form a coherent picture. As Bernal[9] has said, 'The key to the understanding of this chemical evolution of life lies in the junction between observational biochemistry on the one hand and quantum theory on the other', a formidable task indeed! But already it is clear that there are exciting possibilities, and we can begin to discern in matter more clearly than was possible for Tyndall 'the promise and potency of all terrestrial life'.

Supernaturalism. The view that life originated on our planet as a result of a supernatural event which is incapable of description in terms of natural science is a feature of many religions. Beliefs of this kind are not considered, by those who hold them, to be a fit subject for scientific investigation. It is, on the other hand, quite legitimate to ask whether, in the sort of world which we think existed a few thousand million years ago, living things could have arisen without the intervention of a supernatural power, from the continued interaction of different forms of matter and energy. We shall have to leave unanswered the

24

problem of the origin of the universe, a subject on which our ignorance is complete. We can attempt to discover whether, given the sort of universe we know, we can agree with Lucretius that 'Nature, free at once and rid of her haughty lords, is seen to do all things spontaneously of herself, and without the meddling of the gods'.

Lithopanspermia and Radiopanspermia. The suggestion has often been made that life may not have originated on the Earth itself, but that 'seeds' or dormant forms of organisms have in some way been distributed in space, and have grown on any body, such as the Earth, where conditions were suitable.

The adherents of the theory of *lithopanspermia* have suggested that meteorites are the means by which life is transported from one celestial body to another. Numerous attempts have been made to cultivate germs from meteoric fragments, but with an occasional very doubtful exception have given negative results. Investigations of this kind are difficult, as meteoric fragments collected on the Earth may easily have become contaminated with terrestrial micro-organisms.

The theory gained the support of some eminent scientists in the nineteenth century. Lord Kelvin, for example, considered it probable that there were countless seed-bearing stones in space, perhaps originating from collisions of life-bearing planets with other bodies. Helmholtz believed that organisms inside meteorites might be protected sufficiently from the harmful heating effects resulting from passage through the atmosphere, the interior remaining relatively cool although the surface of the meteorite was incandescent. The presence of hydrocarbon compounds in meteorites was thought to be due to the former activities of living organisms; it is now clear that they can be formed by other means, including, for instance, the reaction of metal carbides with other meteoric constituents. A recent report from America has described the detection of the chemical *cytosine* in a meteorite. This is of particular interest because cytosine occurs in living organisms as part of the important nucleic acid molecules (*see* p. 35), and it might be an indication that cytosine can be formed by various reactions in the absence of living things in the course of formation of meteorites. This finding will probably stimulate further examination of the materials present in meteorites, and modern analytical techniques will greatly simplify the task of recognition of compounds which may be present in very small quantities (*see* p. 105).

The great Swedish scientist, Svante Arrhenius, developed the theory of *radiopanspermia*, suggesting that minute germs might be driven from place to place in the universe by radiation pressure. This is physically possible, but it seems likely that an unprotected germ or spore exposed to intense radiations in space would perish in a fairly short time. Arrhenius discussed the possibility that life, matter and energy might be eternal, but did not rule out the possibility of generation of living things from simpler substances in some remote part of the universe.

The theories of lithopanspermia and radiopanspermia are not strictly relevant to the *origin* of life in the universe as a whole, but they must be considered as a possible explanation of the appearance of life on any particular planet. The origin of life separately on individual planets in the Solar System still leaves open the possibility that organisms in some form might be transported from one planet to another, so that the indigenous life of a planet might be supplemented from extraneous sources. At present, final decisions are not possible, but we shall point out, later, ways in which the theories may be tested.

Section II: The Constitution of Living Organisms

Before we can discuss the origin of life, it will be necessary to review briefly the constitution of living things, as we know them on the Earth. It may be thought that a definition of life should be given at this stage, but for various reasons this is not a simple matter, and discussion of the possible form which a definition of life might take will be deferred until later in this section.

Elements in Living Organisms. It has been remarked earlier that the elements constituting living things are all found in inorganic nature. There are no elements which are peculiar to living organisms. The Russian scientist Vinogradov[11, 12] identified about sixty elements which contribute to the formation of organisms, but there are wide variations in the quantities of different elements which are present, and not all of the sixty are found in every kind of organism. Carbon, hydrogen, oxygen, nitrogen, phosphorus and sulphur are invariably found, and sodium, magnesium, chlorine, potassium, calcium and iron, manganese, copper and iodine seem to be invariably present in organisms which are examined. In living material, the atoms present are mostly combined in molecules, some of which are large and complicated, containing tens, hundreds or even thousands of atoms. Some of these important atoms and compounds will now be considered in more detail.

Carbon. The element carbon is an important constituent of all living things which have so far been analysed, and accounts for about 15–20 per cent of the total weight of higher organisms. The formation of many large molecules depends on the ability of carbon atoms to link together to form chains and rings.

The nucleus of the carbon atom consists of 6 protons and 6 neutrons, so that 6 electrons will be necessary to complete the atom (Fig. 3). These 6 electrons are arranged around the nucleus

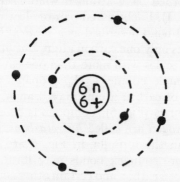

FIG. 3. The Carbon atom.

in two shells, the inner K shell containing 2 electrons and the outer L shell 4. As described earlier (Chapter 1) the K shell can contain at most 2 electrons, and the maximum capacity of the L shell is 8 electrons. In the uncombined carbon atom, the L shell contains 4 electrons, and the nature of this outermost shell largely determines the chemical reactions of carbon, a particular example of a general rule applicable to all atoms.

Methane, or 'marsh gas', is formed by the combination of four hydrogen atoms and one carbon atom (Fig. 4). The four hydrogen atoms contain between them four electrons, which can be shared with the carbon atom. In the resulting compound,

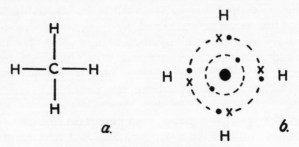

FIG. 4. The Structure of Methane.

a. Conventional Structural Formula.
b. Diagram illustrating electron sharing.
(**x** = Electron from hydrogen atom.
● = Electron from carbon atom.)

methane, CH_4, the carbon atom has, in effect, 8 electrons in the outermost shell, and each hydrogen atom 2 electrons, so that the atoms concerned have attained what is termed 'inert gas structure' (Chap. I). Each shared pair of electrons constitutes a form of chemical bond described as a *covalent bond*. A methane molecule contains only one carbon atom, but other related more complicated molecules with more than one carbon atom can be formed, for example ethane, C_2H_6, propane, C_3H_8 and so on (Fig. 5). Chains of carbon atoms may branch, and rings occur in many compounds (Fig. 5). Compounds consisting wholly of carbon and hydrogen are called *hydrocarbons*. Bonds indicated by single lines in the formulæ in Fig. 5 are known as *single bonds*. Other more complex bonds may form between carbon atoms, and between carbon and certain other elements, and these are called *double* and *triple* bonds, as in ethylene and acetylene respectively (Fig. 6). Compounds which contain double or triple bonds are termed *unsaturated*, and the bonds form relatively reactive sites in the molecules. The types of bonds which we have met here are not the only ones which occur, but they serve to illustrate possible modes of chemical union between elements.

Carbon is a versatile element, and possibilities exist for the formation of enormous numbers of carbon compounds. The

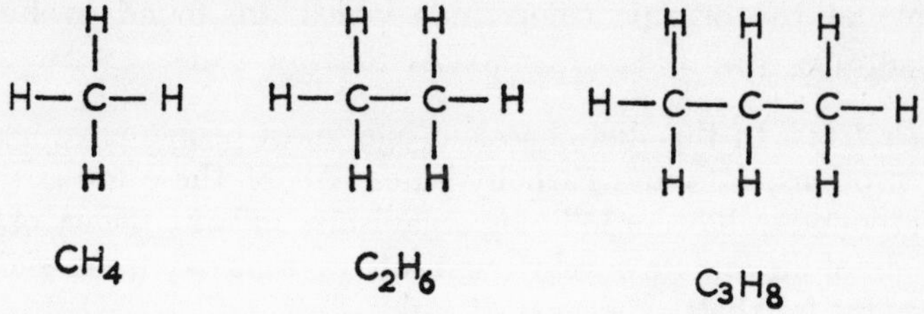

CH_4

a. Methane.

C_2H_6

b. Ethane.

C_3H_8

c. Propane.

C_6H_{12}

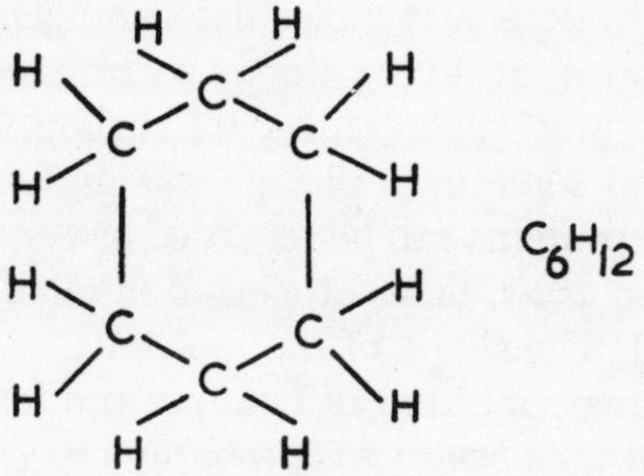

d. Cyclohexane.

FIG. 5. Carbon atoms form chains and rings *

Ethylene, C_2H_4.

Acetylene, C_2H_2.

FIG. 6. Unsaturated Compounds.

study of compounds of carbon constitutes the science of *organic chemistry*. Carbon atoms linked to each other and to other atoms form the backbones of many molecules of biological importance, and at this stage we must turn our attention to

* The simple molecular formulæ (CH_4, C_2H_6, etc.) show the numbers of atoms per molecule, but do not indicate structure. The structural formulæ show how the atoms are arranged, but because they are two-dimensional, the representation is necessarily limited. Three-dimensional molecular models can give a truer picture.

some of the organic compounds which are found in living organisms.

Proteins. In this diet-conscious age, most people have heard of proteins, fats and carbohydrates. All of these are carbon compounds, all occur in living organisms, and any theory of the origin of life and its development into present-day forms should account for their existence.

Proteins form a class of complicated chemical compounds with a similar underlying structural pattern, but the individual proteins differ in details of molecular arrangements. Examples have been found in all living things so far examined. The elements found in protein molecules are carbon, hydrogen, nitrogen, oxygen and sometimes phosphorus and sulphur. Analysis has shown that proteins can be regarded as consisting of simpler units, the *amino-acids*, linked together in chains which may be folded or coiled. The shape of the molecules is probably partly dependent on a special kind of bonding produced by hydrogen atoms. This *hydrogen bonding* is probably an electrostatic effect, the positive proton of the small hydrogen atom being sufficiently exposed to be able to attract and link certain other atoms; because of this, hydrogen bonding is sometimes called *proton bonding*. Hydrogen bonds are weak, having only about 10 per cent of the strength of the chemical bonds described earlier. They play an important part in compounds other than proteins, the structure of water and nucleic acids partly determined by forces of this kind, as will be described later.

The simplest amino-acid is *glycine*, and *alanine* is somewhat more complicated (Fig. 7). Altogether, about 20 amino acids are important as building blocks for the proteins of living organ-

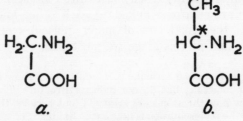

FIG. 7. *a*. Glycine.   *b*. Alanine.

isms. Examination of the formulæ for glycine and alanine will show a difference between them. In alanine, the carbon atom marked C* has four different chemical groups attached to it: —CH$_3$, —NH$_2$, —H and —COOH. In glycine, there is no carbon atom with four different attached groups. A carbon atom of the type marked C* is called an *asymmetric* carbon atom, and it is possible to obtain two distinct forms of a compound which contains an asymmetric carbon atom, related to each other as mirror images. In two dimensions on paper, the molecular forms can be represented as in Fig. 8. The nomenclature L(+) and D(−) is

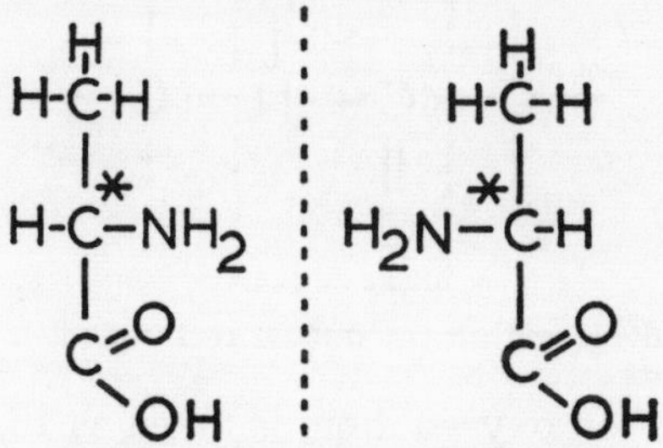

FIG. 8. 'Mirror-image' molecules.

used to distinguish these forms, and for the present it is sufficient to note that the (+) and (−) indicate that solutions of these forms of the compounds will rotate the plane of polarized light to the right and left respectively. The existence of two molecular forms, made up of the same number of atoms arranged differently, is an example of chemical *isomerism*, and since the particular molecules we have considered influence the behaviour of polarized light, they are called *optical isomers*. The common amino-acids found in the proteins of living organisms belong to the L series, but in micro-organisms, some of the D series occur. There is, however, a great preponderance of L forms in living things, and we shall discuss the possible reasons for this later. All the amino acids except glycine display the phenomenon of optical isomerism. Since one optical isomer rotates the plane of polarized light to the right and the other to the left, a mixture of the two forms in equal proportions will be optically inactive, and is termed the *racemic* form. The existence of optical isomerism in chemical compounds was first elucidated in the nineteenth

century by Louis Pasteur, whose work on spontaneous generation was mentioned earlier. Pasteur was responsible for fundamental advances in microbiology and chemistry, and in the
medical applications of bacteriology. Bernal[13] has given a fascinating account of Pasteur's investigation of the isomerism of
tartaric acid.

In proteins, the amino-acid 'building blocks' are linked by the
formation of *peptide bonds* (Fig. 9). Proteins have high molecular
weights, and contain many amino-acid units in each molecule.

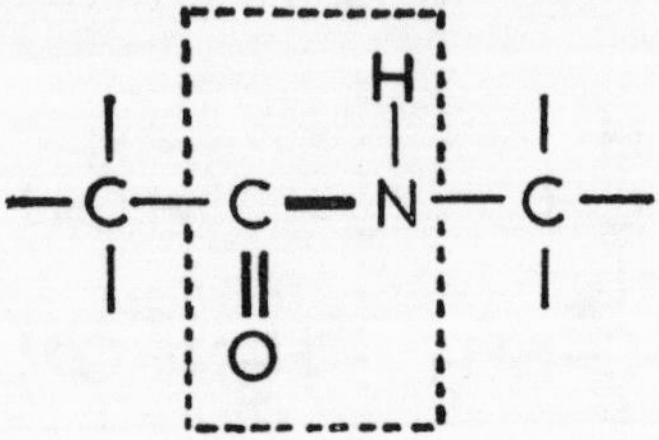

FIG. 9. The linkage within the dotted rectangle is a 'peptide bond'.

If the weight of an oxygen atom is taken as 16, the molecular
weight of glycine on the same scale is 71, that of the protein
hæmoglobin, in blood, about 68,000, and a protein called

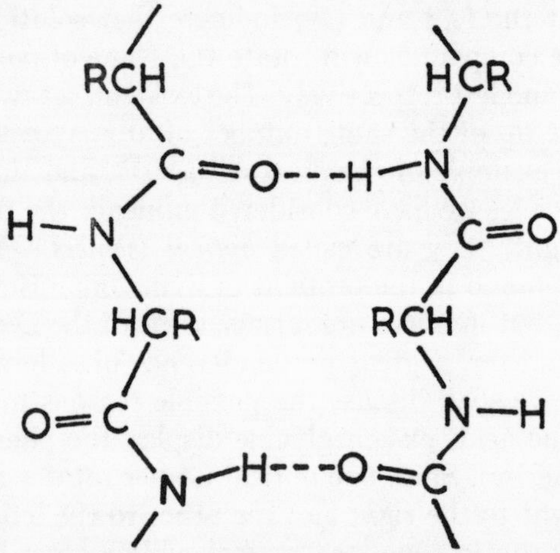

FIG. 10. Part of a protein molecule. R = Chemical groups not shown in
full. - - - between H and O atoms = Hydrogen bonds.

hæmocyanin, found in snails, has a molecular weight of about 5,000,000. It is not merely the number of atoms in protein molecules which is important. The properties of any particular protein are determined by the arrangement of the constituent atoms. The form of protein molecules can be radically altered by exposure to various chemical reagents, such as acids and alkalis, and by heating or exposure to radiations. These effects place important limitations on the range of conditions which can be tolerated by living organisms.

Carbohydrates. In various forms, carbohydrates are used extensively in daily life. Cane sugar and glucose are fairly simple carbohydrates. Starch is a more complicated one, a *polysaccharide*, and this name implies that starch molecules are built up from many sugar, or *saccharide* molecules. Carbohydrates consist of carbon, hydrogen and oxygen atoms joined together,

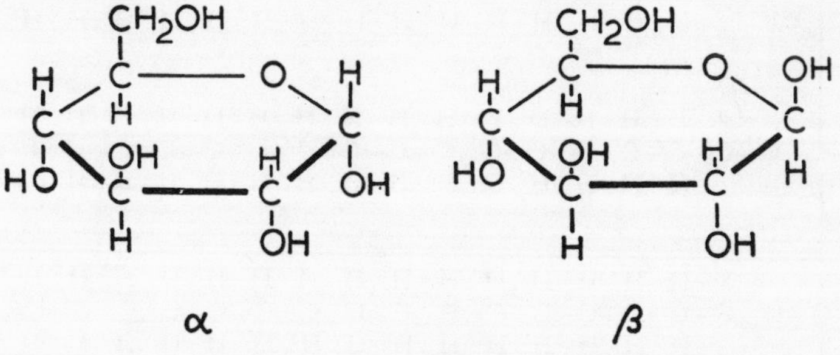

FIG. 11. Structural formulæ of α- and β-glucose.

the ratio of the numbers of hydrogen atoms to oxygen atoms in each molecule being $2:1$. A molecule of glucose contains 6 carbon atoms, 12 hydrogen atoms and 6 oxygen atoms, so that using conventional chemical symbols we can denote the glucose molecule by the formula $C_6H_{12}O_6$. A formula of this kind tells us the number of atoms in each molecule, but gives no idea of the arrangement of the atoms. Many different sugar molecules may be made up of the same number of atoms arranged in slightly different patterns. To depict these differences, more elaborate formulæ must be written; these are *structural formulae*, and give, as the name implies, some idea of the details of molecular structure. Glucose, for instance, can exist as ring structures known as alpha- and beta-glucose, and the structural formulae are shown in Fig. 11.

The chemistry of carbohydrates is complicated, and many subtle variations of molecular structure are possible. Polysaccharide molecules are large, and may consist of hundreds of sugar units linked together. Starch is produced by plants, and in animals a rather similar but not identical polysaccharide, glycogen, is found. The wide range of different sugars produced by various species of living things and built into the structure of their tissues is an indication of the importance of these compounds for present-day organisms.

Fats. These form another series of compounds with molecules built up from carbon, hydrogen and oxygen atoms, and as with

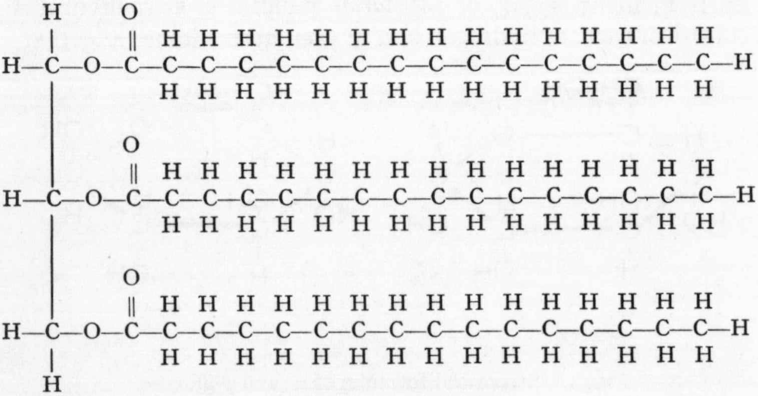

FIG. 12. A fat molecule.

other compounds, the properties of fats are determined by the arrangement of the constituent atoms. The structural formula of a typical fat is shown in Fig. 12.

Nucleic Acids. Living things grow, and from time to time multiply. In order to grow they must be able to build up more molecules similar to those of which they are composed; food is the source of material for these molecules. When organisms multiply, new individuals more or less resembling the parent or parents are produced, and this requires some method of duplication of structure. It is becoming clear that certain substances called *nucleic acids* play important rôles in processes of growth and reproduction, and that the forms of their molecules in some way determine the production of the correct new molecules.

The bodies of living organisms consist of small *cells*, and these can be examined microscopically. The smallest organisms consist of a single cell, whereas the body of a man contains many billions of cells. Cells differ considerably in size in different organisms and in different situations in the same organism, and different types of cell perform special functions in complicated organisms. There are in a man, for example, muscle cells, brain cells, blood cells, liver cells and so on. The diameters of cells are commonly about $\frac{1}{100}$ to $\frac{1}{20}$ mm., but there are wide differences in shape, some being of great length in proportion to their width. Microscopically, each cell is seen to consist of a dense central region, or *nucleus*, surrounded by an outer zone, the *cytoplasm*. The cytoplasm contains granules of various kinds, and some of these are complicated structures responsible for handling foods and building up new compounds.

Two main kinds of nucleic acid have been identified, *deoxyribonucleic acid* (DNA) and *ribonucleic acid* (RNA). The DNA is a constituent of cell nuclei, and ribonucleic acid is found in components of the cytoplasm as well as in the nucleus. DNA seems to be of fundamental importance in the determination of cell form, and is closely concerned in hereditary mechanisms, while the cytoplasmic RNA probably plays an important part in the synthesis (building up) of new proteins. In modern terms, the nucleic acids are stores of 'information', ensuring that the correct new molecules are made from molecules which have been derived from foods. The ability to store information depends on the structural form of the nucleic acid molecules, and the structure of DNA has excited particular interest among biochemists during the past few years.

Like proteins, nucleic acids have giant molecules which can be analysed into simpler units. The elements in nucleic acid molecules are carbon, hydrogen, oxygen, nitrogen and phosphorus. The DNA molecule has a 'backbone' of sugar units linked by phosphate groups, the sugar being *deoxyribose*, whereas in RNA the sugar is *ribose*. This backbone has attached to it side-groups, which may be one of four substances, the bases adenine, cytosine, guanine and thymine (Fig. 13). These bases are attached to the sugar units of the molecule in irregular order. Recent investigations[14, 15] have shown that the molecules of DNA probably have a spiral, or helical shape, each molecule

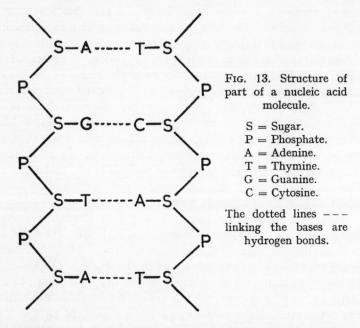

Fig. 13. Structure of part of a nucleic acid molecule.

S = Sugar.
P = Phosphate.
A = Adenine.
T = Thymine.
G = Guanine.
C = Cytosine.

The dotted lines – – – linking the bases are hydrogen bonds.

consisting of a pair of DNA chains 'wound' around a common axis and linked together by the protruding bases (Fig. 14). The pairs of bases at each linking point are either adenine and thymine, or guanine and cytosine. The linkage between the base is by hydrogen bonding, a relatively weak linkage as compared with other bonds in the molecule, as we saw when discussing protein molecules.

When a cell divides into two, there must be duplication of the various structures, including the nucleic acids. It seems likely that the double spiral can untwist; and that as it does so, a new strand is built up on each half. Thus the two halves of the original molecule act as 'patterns' for the new strands, determining the arrangements of the components. There is evidence, too, that the DNA of the nucleus controls, among other things, the kind

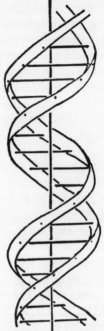

FIG. 14. Spiral form of DNA molecule.

of RNA made in the cell, and that this in turn carries the necessary 'information' for the production of the correct kinds of protein.

A cell is not just a bag of mixed chemicals, but a functioning system of interrelated components. Incoming foods, sources of energy and materials, are changed by ordered reaction sequences into the molecules required for growth.

Viruses. It is convenient at this point to mention viruses which from one point of view may be regarded as incomplete organisms. They are minute particles of protein and nucleic acid, and if they gain entry to suitable cells they may be replicated, and affect cell function in various ways. The status of viruses in the biological hierarchy is uncertain, but they are unable to reproduce except inside living cells. The resulting disturbances of cell function may give rise to disease in man, animals and plants. Poliomyelitis, mumps and influenza, for example, are virus diseases. There is little point in arguing about whether or not viruses are 'alive', as will become evident when we discuss the difficulty of defining life.

Energy of Activation and Chemical Reactions. Enzymes

Atoms or molecules in a mixture are only able to react if they reach a certain energy level, when they are said to be in the *activated state*. The energy necessary for the activation of the reactants may be obtained from various sources, for instance heat or ultra-violet radiation.

It is frequently found that the energy of activation for a reaction between two substances is reduced if a third substance is introduced into the reaction mixture, although the third substance does not undergo permanent change in the course of the reaction. This is the phenomenon of *catalysis*, and the substance

37

which leads to acceleration of reaction rate without itself being lost in the course of the reaction is termed a *catalyst*. Large numbers of substances act as catalysts for chemical reactions, so that catalysis is a fairly general phenomenon in chemistry, and has important applications in experimental and industrial processes. Catalysts act by intervening in some way in the reaction, forming transient linkages with the reactant molecules and so modifying the energy requirements. After this transient change, the catalyst is restored to its former state.

In chemical evolution, a special rôle may have been played by the process of *autocatalysis*. If two substances react to give certain products, it is sometimes found that one of the products itself acts as a catalyst for the reaction, and so, as this product is formed, the rate of reaction increases. Calvin[16] has discussed the possible importance of autocatalysis for the evolution of chemicals leading to the origin of life.

Living organisms contain a special class of catalysts which enable them to carry out reactions which would otherwise proceed slowly or hardly at all at ordinary temperatures. These special catalysts are called *enzymes* and always, so far as is known, consist of protein molecules, often associated with other smaller molecules called *co-enzymes*. Whereas simple catalysts, such as manganese dioxide, may speed many different chemical reactions, enzymes display a considerable degree of specificity. A particular enzyme may be effective for increasing the rate of reaction of only certain specific chemicals or groups of chemicals. This feature of enzymes is of great importance for the efficient organization of the chains of chemical reactions which proceed inside living cells. Certain enzymes speed certain reactions, but not others, so that the cell can exist as a system of ordered, interlinked reaction chains, and is not merely a muddle of reactions non-specifically catalysed in a random manner.

Other 'Biological' Molecules. In the processes of cell *metabolism*—a general term for the building up and breaking down processes in the living cell—certain molecules are particularly concerned with energy storage and transfer. It is not possible to discuss any of these in detail, but examples will be mentioned to give some idea of the structures and processes involved in the flow and utilization of energy. The functioning organism may be regarded as an example of an *open system*[2, 17]. Food is taken in and waste products are discharged; the inflow of food supplies the materials and energy for life, but the food has to be altered and used for building up new parts. The organism is at the same time wearing out and reconstituting itself. It is an open system because it continually exchanges materials and energy with its surroundings, and death is marked by cessation of this process of interchange. Special molecules take part in the energy transformations of life.

Adenosine Triphosphate (ATP). During metabolic processes in cells, energy is stored for a time in special 'high energy' chemical bonds which are formed in certain phosphorus-containing organic molecules. ATP is an excellent example, and is widespread in living organisms. The molecule may be represented as in Fig. 15.

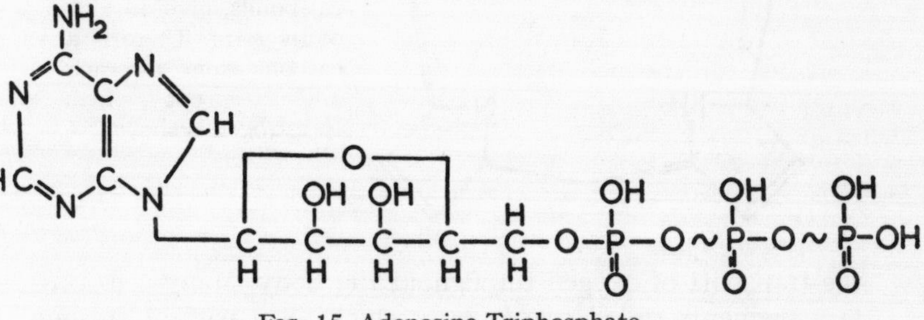

FIG. 15. Adenosine Triphosphate.

The bonds indicated by the sign $\sim$ are the high-energy bonds. ATP takes part in various reactions in which phosphate groups are transferred to other molecules, and these transferences are accompanied by release of energy which is used by the cell. In the course of metabolism, ATP is repeatedly handing on phosphate groups to various compounds and then being re-formed by acquisition of phosphate from other sources.

It is possible that simpler phosphate-containing compounds capable of analogous exchange mechanisms were developed at an early stage in chemical evolution, and it has been suggested by Lipmann[18] that carbamyl phosphate, $OC \cdot NH_2 \cdot OPO_3$, may be regarded as the first 'living molecule', a first step in bio-chemical evolution.

Porphyrins. The members of this group of chemically related substances are responsible for important processes in cells. The molecules are variations on the basic structure *porphin* (Fig. 16). There are several different porphyrins, and in their functional forms they are usually combined with a metal and a protein to form highly active compounds. An iron-porphyrin combination is found in the hæmoglobin of blood, which is responsible for

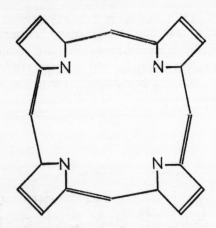

FIG. 16. 'Skeleton' of the Porphin molecule. The molecule is not shown in full, but the lines, indicating chemical bonds, give an idea of its form. There is a carbon atom at each angle, except where nitrogen is shown.

the transport of oxygen throughout the body. Many cells contain pigments called *cytochromes*, which form part of enzyme systems concerned with the respiration of cells, and these are metal-porphyrin-protein compounds chemically related to hæmoglobin. The enzyme *catalase*, which is widely distributed in living organisms, can break down hydrogen peroxide to water and oxygen, and is another example of an iron-porphyrin compound. The iron combined in the catalase is essential for the combination of hydrogen peroxide with the enzyme. Ions of inorganic iron have some activity in breaking down hydrogen peroxide to water and oxygen, but it has been calculated one milligramme of iron combined in catalase has an activity about equal to that of ten tons of inorganic iron. Calvin[16] has used this as an illustration of his view that the fundamental character of the enzymes of present-day living organisms results from the evolutionary development of rudimentary powers of catalysis of simple ions or molecules of the prebiological environment.

The chlorophyll of green plants is a metal-porphyrin compound, (Fig. 17), but here the metal is magnesium and not iron.

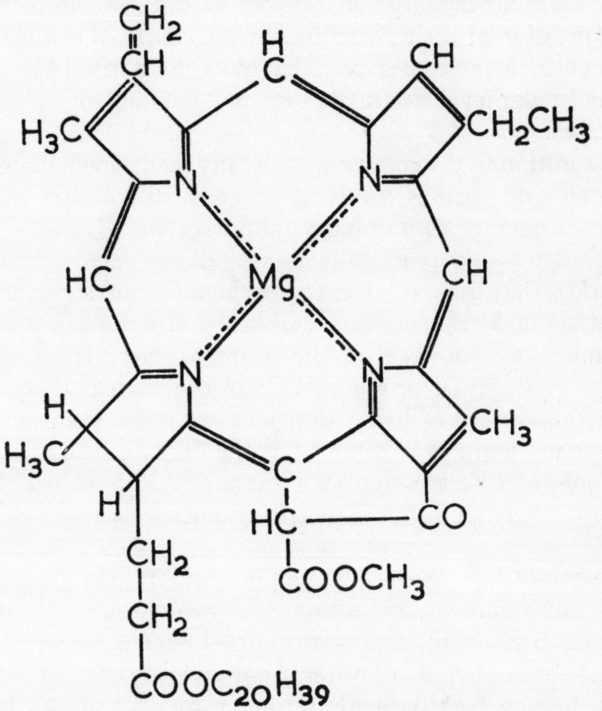

FIG. 17. Molecule of Chlorophyll a, of plants.

Chlorophyll helps to trap the energy of sunlight and make it available for metabolic processes. Calvin[16] has pointed out that iron would be unsuitable for this purpose. After chlorophyll has captured a quantum of solar energy, a long-lived excitation is necessary for its functioning, but the magnetic nature of the iron atom would preclude this. Magnesium can have a long-lived excitation, and so mediate energy migration and conversion with a high degree of efficiency.

Porphyrins are found as numerous other pigments in nature,

for example the copper-porphyrin *turacin* in the feathers of the Turaco bird, and the copper-containing *hæmocyanins* which act as oxygen carriers in molluscs. We can see how subtle variations on a chemical theme can lead to the production of fundamentally related but functionally different compounds. We can appreciate, too, that the functional capacities of these compounds are an expression of their structure. In the course of evolution, the most efficient molecules available have, by natural selection at the molecular level, gradually become predominant in biological processes.

In addition to the compounds already mentioned, many other molecules of various kinds are widely distributed in living things. Enzymes containing vitamins of the B group, for instance, are found practically universally in cells. Bernal[18] has remarked that there is 'an extreme chemical and structural conservatism or inertia of once established structure or activities. At and above the level of the protozoa there is no essential change in structure or metabolism of the nucleated cell.'

All the variety of living things as we know them on Earth share many features in common at the fundamental level of cell metabolism. Life is a symphony composed of related themes, and not a medley of unrelated fragments.

Water and Life. Water plays an essential rôle in the processes of life as we know it, and although some organisms can survive for long periods in a dormant, dried state, active living is dependent on a supply of water. About 60 per cent of the weight of the human body is made up by water. We are all familiar with water, because it covers about 70 per cent of the Earth's surface, but perhaps we do not often think of the remarkable properties of the commonest liquid found under natural conditions on our planet.

Ice floats on water, and water is the only substance known which is less dense in its solid than in its liquid state. This property is of vital importance to aquatic creatures, because the layer of ice which forms on the surface of water acts as an insulator against rapid cooling of the deeper layers. Consequently, rivers and lakes do not usually freeze solid, and living things can survive in the water beneath the ice.

The water molecule is usually represented by the formula H_2O, which implies that it consists of two atoms of hydrogen combined with one of oxygen. This formula is a gross over-simplification, as was hinted earlier when we were considering hydrogen bonds. The hydrogen atom, it will be remembered, consists of a proton with one orbiting electron, whereas the oxygen atom has electrons arranged around the nucleus in two shells, an inner with two electrons and an outer with six. The electrons of two hydrogen atoms can 'fit' into the outer shell of an oxygen atom, to form the classical water molecule H_2O (Fig. 18), but in water, molecules of this kind do not remain

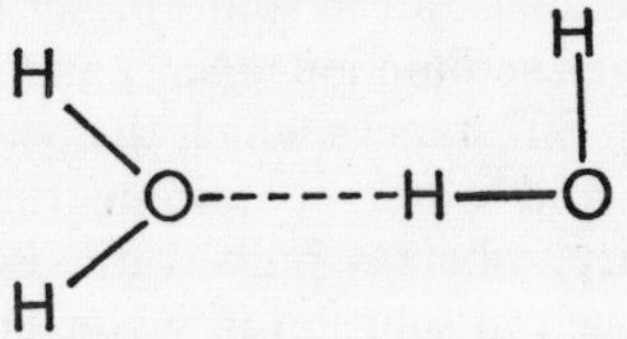

FIG. 18. Water molecules associating. – – – = Hydrogen bond.

separate in a higgledy-piggledy manner. Instead, each hydrogen atom is attracted towards another oxygen atom by the formation of a hydrogen bond, so that water can be described as a 'united association' rather than as a mixture of molecules.[19] The presence of hydrogen bonds causes water to absorb infra-red radiation very strongly.

The composition of water is further complicated by the presence of traces of other components formed from isotopes of oxygen and hydrogen. The three isotopes of oxygen, O^{16}, O^{17} and O^{18} (the figures indicate atomic weights) can combine with the three hydrogen isotopes, hydrogen, deuterium and tritium to give eighteen different molecules, and these molecules can, by loss of electrons, form fifteen different ions. This means that water contains thirty-three different components, but of these the combinations of ordinary hydrogen and oxygen are present in vastly greater amount than the others.

Heavy water, D_2O, is present in water to the extent of about one part in 5000. Its freezing and boiling points are rather higher than those of ordinary water. Mice have been rendered sterile by the addition of 30 per cent D_2O to their drinking water, and it may inhibit the reproduction of algæ and growth of some tumours.

The arrangement of atoms in ice is regular, but in liquid water it is more disorderly. More than two hydrogen atoms may be joined with one oxygen atom, and a single hydrogen atom may be surrounded by as many as three oxygen atoms sharing hydrogen bonds. The hydrogen atoms are not static, but move in a chain-like fashion from molecule to molecule.

Water is an excellent solvent for many substances, so the preparation of really pure water is exceedingly difficult. Many molecules, when dissolved in water, dissociate into positively and negatively charged ions. Salt in solution, for example, is present as positively charged sodium ions (Na^+) and negatively charged chloride ions (Cl^-). Substances which dissociate in this way are called *electrolytes*, and water containing them is a good conductor of electricity, whereas pure water is an insulator. The ions can exist as such in solution in water because the positive ions are neutralized by oxygen atoms, and the negative ions by hydrogen atoms.

Water is a major component of living things. In addition to forming a medium for chemical reactions, it takes part in reactions itself and has a profound effect on the detailed organization of living matter.

Photosynthesis. The Sun is the ultimate source of energy for living organisms, and the trapping of solar energy is achieved by plants and by some other organisms which contain special chemical systems able to perform this feat. It is likely that oxygen released in the course of these *photosynthetic* processes accounts for the abundance of free oxygen in our atmosphere today. In a few thousand years, there is an almost complete 'turn-over' of atmospheric oxygen; Rabinowitch[20] has stated that each year the plants of the Earth combine about 150 billion tons of carbon with 25 billion tons of hydrogen and set free 400 billion tons of oxygen. It has been estimated that about 90 per cent of the total photosynthesis on Earth is carried out not by land plants, but by algæ living in the sea. Plants are able to use solar energy to help drive chemical reactions leading to the production of more complicated molecules from carbon dioxide and water. Animals rely on plants to do this, so there is an energy 'chain' from the Sun to plants, and thence to herbivorous, omnivorous and carnivorous animals (Fig. 19).

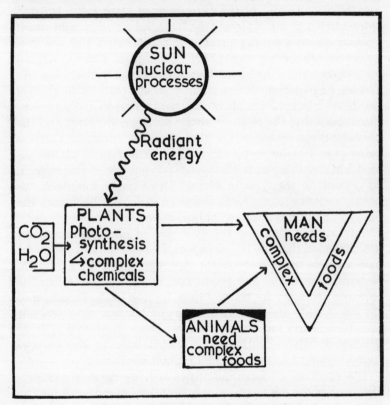

FIG. 19. Energy chain from Sun to Man.

The basic reaction of photosynthesis appears to be the splitting of water molecules by light—the *photolysis* of water. As a result, hydrogen is made available and this reacts with carbon dioxide to give molecules which form the starting point for building up more complicated compounds. The carbon dioxide is chemically *reduced* by the hydrogen. The oxygen of the water finally appears as the free gas, and the oxygen released by plants comes exclusively from water.

Plants trap solar energy by means of their chlorophyll (Fig.

18), but the process may also be assisted by other pigments, known as *carotenoids*. In plants, the chlorophyll and associated pigments are bound in bodies called *chloroplasts*, which can be seen microscopically in the cytoplasm of plant cells. Isolated chlorophyll, removed from the chloroplast, does not itself photosynthesize, as the process is complicated and involves numerous other components of the chloroplast. Chlorophyll is a vital energy-transformer in the system. Some bacteria contain a chlorophyll which differs slightly in structure from that of plants, and, as in plants, there may be other associated pigments. Fundamentally, the photosynthetic processes in plants and the photosynthetic bacteria are the same, the primary reaction being photolysis of water followed by reduction of carbon dioxide; but, unlike plants, the bacteria do not release free oxygen. As a result of reactions involving, for example, hydrogen sulphide, various organic acids and even molecular hydrogen, the oxygen finally emerges recombined as water.[21]

Calvin[16] has discussed the evolution of photosynthesis and has suggested that the beginnings of the chlorophyll type might have occurred very early in the development of life on Earth, perhaps even before the production of the earliest cells. The enzymes necessary for the reactions leading to the reduction of carbon dioxide are present in many organisms which do not themselves carry out photosynthesis. These enzymes may have developed independently, and coupled later to the energy-capturing and transforming chlorophyll mechanism.

The existence of large quantities of free oxygen in a planetary atmosphere might reasonably be taken as evidence for the existence of photosynthetic organisms on the planet. Primary splitting of water by ultra-violet light releases free oxygen, but it is unlikely that this alone could produce and maintain the concentration we find in our atmosphere. On the other hand, the absence of oxygen would not necessarily rule out the existence of photosynthetic organisms, for as we have seen, not all types release free oxygen.

Entropy and Life. Entropy may be described as a measure of the disorganization of a system. The second law of thermodynamics states that entropy always increases, so that entropy can be used as an indicator of the passage of time. If we know that at time t_1 the entropy of a system was less than at time t_2, then t_2 was later in time than t_1. Eddington[22] has emphasized that when entropy is used as a 'signpost' for time in this way, it is necessary to take care that a properly isolated system is being considered, for a system can gain organization by 'draining it from contiguous systems'.

When organisms grow and develop, they apparently gain organization, and it has sometimes been suggested that they defy the second law of thermodynamics and so lie outside the realm of physics. That this is not so has become clear. Organisms gain organization only when they can take in food and use the energy stored in it, and plants can use the energy of sunlight. An organism does not remain active if deprived of energy supplies. As Eddington has said, if we cut off a man's food, drink and air, 'he will ere long come to a state which everyone would recognize as a state of extreme "disorganization" '. In the words of Schrödinger,[23] organisms feed on 'negative entropy', and if we trace back the energy chain from animals to plants, we find that plants use solar energy and that it is the organized solar radiations which provide the necessary energy, the 'negative entropy', for the vital processes of organisms. In isolation, organisms obey the second law of thermodynamics, and it does not seem necessary to postulate 'vital forces' of a non-physical kind to account for the local entropy decrease in the functioning organism.

Can Life be Defined? Many attempts have been made to frame a brief and satisfactory definition of life, and all have failed. It seems that no matter what list of properties we draw up as characteristic of living things, exceptions are always found. Movement is not peculiar to living things, and neither is growth, for crystals grow. There is general agreement that some things— active human beings, dogs, cats, growing plants—are 'alive', but when we consider viruses, which are reproduced only within living cells, there is plenty of room for argument and little hope of agreement. Pirie[24], in an article entitled 'The meaninglessness of the terms "Life" and "Living" ', argued that until a valid definition has been framed, it is prudent to avoid the use of the word 'life' in any discussion about borderline systems, and to refrain from saying that certain observations on a system have proved that it is or is not 'alive'.

Bernal[9] has more recently tentatively suggested that, if we limit ourselves to a consideration of the 'life' accessible to our observation on this Earth, 'we can for the moment find one common characteristic, the presence of protein molecules, and ... one common physico-chemical process, the stepwise catalysis of organic compounds carried out practically isothermally by quantum jumps of between 3 and 16 kilo-calories, small compared with the usual jumps of 300 in laboratory chemistry'. This may point the way to a type of meaningful definition.

Horowitz[25] has proposed that living things are characterized by three properties, ability to duplicate, to influence their environment in a way which insures a supply of materials necessary for their perpetuation, and an ability to mutate randomly and reproduce in the new form. On this view, even certain types of complex molecules would be termed 'alive', but the suggestion has met with much criticism.

There seems little point in attempting to draw up precise definitions at the present time. Perhaps, when more detailed knowledge has been obtained, a useful definition will be possible. Fortunately, as Pauling[26] has remarked, 'it is sometimes easier to study a subject than to define it'.

Section III: Pathways to Life

Living things are not just mixtures of different chemicals, but dynamic systems in which the parts interact. They are to some extent self-regulating, but at the same time depend on the existence of a suitable range of environmental conditions. The surroundings must not be too hot or too cold, and the correct foods must be available. In the course of ages, many different organisms have evolved, and some can tolerate, and may even require, conditions which would be fatal to others.

What now of the possible modes of origin of living things from inorganic materials? We must try to decide whether, in the course of time, simple and then more complicated organisms might have been produced in an evolutionary sequence starting from the materials of the primitive earth. The term 'biopœsis', suggested by Pirie,[27] will be used for the process of production of living from non-living matter. We must consider whether the conditions which are believed to have existed on the Earth two or three thousand million years ago could have started the chain of events which has led to the variety of living things we find today. Was the origin of life the result of some isolated and highly improbable association and reaction of chemicals at some point on the Earth, or was it a straightforward consequence of the way chemicals behave, one stage following another as surely as night follows day? Is life on the Earth an example of an exceedingly rare phenomenon in the cosmos, or shall we be able to conclude that other planets more or less similar to the Earth in composition and conditions are probably the homes of life?

At the meeting of the British Association in Dundee, in 1912, E. A. Schäfer[28] spoke of the origin of life from the evolutionary standpoint: 'Looking, therefore, at the evolution of living matter by the light which is shed upon it by the study of the evolution of matter in general, we are led to regard it as having been produced, not by a sudden alteration, whether exerted by a natural or supernatural agency, but by a gradual process of change from material which was lifeless, through material on the borderland between the animate and the inanimate to material which has all the characteristics to which we attach the term "life".' Schäfer was careful to make it clear that, at the time, there was no certain knowledge of the mode of this transformation. At about the same time, a short book on the origin of life was written by Benjamin Moore,[29] Professor of Biochemistry in Liverpool. Moore wrote that 'It was no fortuitous combination of chances, and no cosmic dust, which brought life to the womb of our ancient mother earth in the far distant Palæozoic ages, but a well-regulated orderly development, which comes to every mother earth in the Universe in the maturity of her creation when the conditions arrive within the suitable limits'. These statements typify the spirit of much recent thought in this field.

The Theories of Haldane and Oparin. During the 1920's, two scientists, J. B. S. Haldane in England and A. I. Oparin in the

U.S.S.R., were thinking and writing about the origin of life. Working independently, they arrived at rather similar conclusions, so that the term 'Haldane-Oparin Theory' is sometimes used, when referring to their views.

Haldane's essay on the origin of life[30] contains a summary of his position. He suggested that the Earth's primitive atmosphere probably contained little or no oxygen, because the present supply of oxygen is only about the amount necessary to burn all the coal and other organic remains found on and below the surface. On the other hand, Haldane thought it likely that there was much more carbon dioxide in the primitive atmosphere than there is now, and that much of the nitrogen now free in the atmosphere was combined as nitride in the Earth's crust. There would have been free ammonia in the atmosphere as a result of the action of water on the metal nitrides. At the present time, much of the short wave ultra-violet radiation from the Sun is filtered off by ozone (a form of oxygen) in our atmosphere. Before there was much free oxygen, this filtering layer would have been almost absent, so that more ultra-violet radiation would have reached the surface of the Earth.

Even before 1929, when Haldane's essay appeared, Baly, of Liverpool, had shown that when ultra-violet radiations act on a mixture of water, carbon dioxide and ammonia, simple organic chemicals may be formed, including, probably, simple amino-acids. Haldane, therefore, had some experimental backing for the further suggestion that similar processes in the primitive atmosphere might have led to the accumulation of organic compounds in the oceans of the Earth until they 'reached the consistency of hot, dilute soup'. Whereas, today, an organism must compete with others for food, the precursors of life would have been formed in a rich, chemical soup, and would have found 'food' all around them. It is clear, too, that the earliest organisms would not, under these conditions, have had free oxygen to use.

We have mentioned earlier that many organisms exist which can live in the absence of free oxygen, and indeed some are unable to grow in its presence. Organisms which live without oxygen are called *anaerobes*, and obtain their energy from foods by the process of 'fermentation', termed by Pasteur 'life without

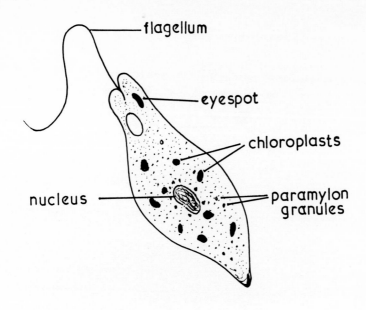

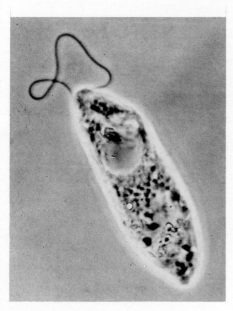

1. *Euglena gracilis*. This interesting organism (about $\frac{1}{20}$ mm. long) may be regarded as consisting of a single cell. It contains chloroplasts, and in light can carry on a plant type of photosynthesis. In the dark, it can live on more complex organic molecules, and so in this respect resembles animals. There are other examples of this combination of 'plant' and 'animal' features among micro-organisms. Found in pond water. *Above:* Diagram of typical Euglena. *Left:* Photograph of living Euglena.

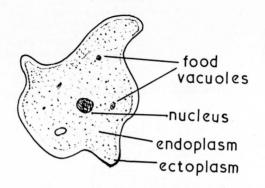

food
vacuoles

nucleus

endoplasm

ectoplasm

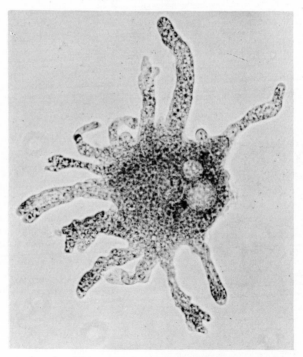

2. *Amœba*. This organism, larger than Euglena, is a
tiny 'animal'. It does not contain chloroplasts and is
unable to use light energy directly. It requires complex foods. Found in pond water. *Above:* Diagram of
a typical Amœba. *Below:* Photograph of a living
Amœba.

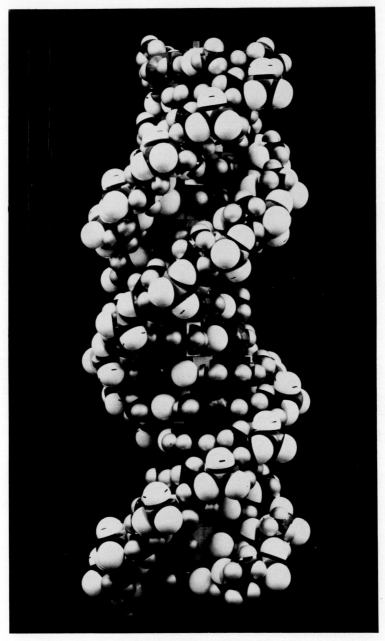

3. Model of DNA Molecule. The various atoms are represented by spheres.

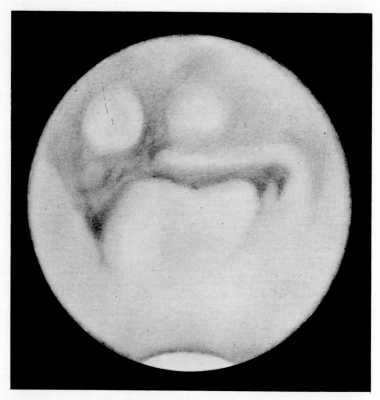

4. Mars. Drawing by L. F. Ball. 1958 December 1st. G.M.A.T., 19½ hours. Longitude of C.M. 331°. Instrument—10in. reflector × 300. Image telescopically inverted. The dark v-shaped Syrtis Major is well shown. Above (i.e., south of) Syrtis Major is the white area of Hellas. Extending from the Syrtis Major is the Sirius Sabæus, above which is a second white area, Noachis; the dark strip between Hellas and Noachis is the Hellespontus. The North Polar Cap is prominently shown.

5. Venus. 200-in. photograph, Mount Wilson and Palomar Observatories.

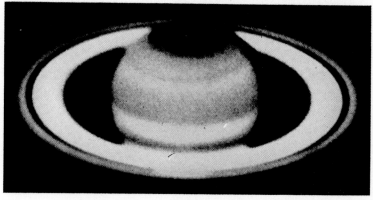

6. Saturn. Flagstaff Observatory photograph.

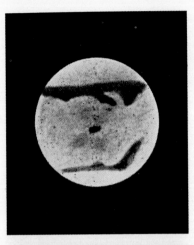

7. Drawings of Mars by Patrick Moore showing the axial rotation of the planet.

1960 Dec. 29. 19·05 × 300. 8½ inch reflector. $\omega = 203\cdot2$.

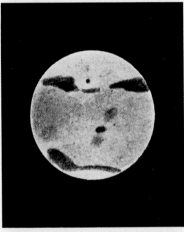

1961 Jan. 11. 19·45 × 300. 8½ inch reflector. $\omega = 098\cdot7$.

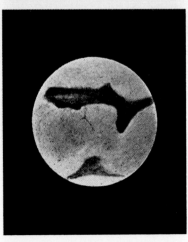

1961 Feb. 6. 22·20 × 525. 24 inch reflector. $\omega = 264\cdot7$.

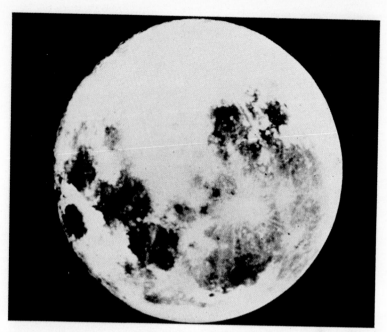

8. The Moon, almost full.

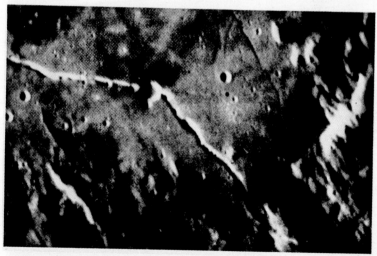

9. The Hyginus Cleft, photographed at the Pic du Midi. The 'cleft' is really, in part, a crater-chain.

10. Cluster of Galaxies in Coma Berenices. 200-in. photograph, Mount Wilson and Palomar Observatories.

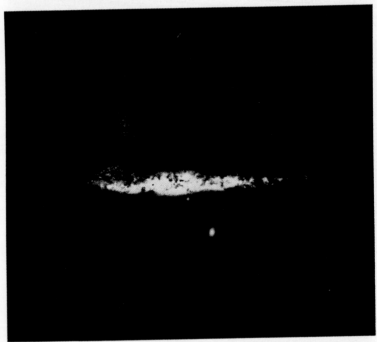

11. Galaxy N.G.C. 4361, in Canes Venatici: this is a spiral, but is seen edge-on. 200-in. photograph, Mount Wilson and Palomar Observatories.

oxygen'. Some bacteria can live in the presence or absence of free oxygen. The cells of organisms which require oxygen still contain the necessary enzymes for carrying out fermentations. It is as if the more primitive fermentation mechanisms have been supplemented by oxygen-requiring systems in the course of evolution. Organisms which use free oxygen to 'burn' their foods can obtain much more energy from a given quantity of food than organisms which rely on fermentations alone, so that oxygen-requiring, or *aerobic* organisms, are more efficient than the anaerobes in this respect. It has recently been suggested by Nursall[31, 32] that free oxygen in the atmosphere was a prerequisite to the origin of many-celled organisms (metazoa).

Oparin first expressed his views on the origin of life at a meeting of the Russian Botanical Society in 1922, and a short account of them[33] was published in 1924. More recently, he has developed his theories at greater length in publications which are available in English translation.[34, 2, 35, 36, 37] Haldane had thought that carbon dioxide (CO_2) was the most likely form in which carbon was present in the primitive atmosphere, but Oparin suggested that methane (CH_4) was more probable. Which of these two views is correct remains uncertain, but there is fairly general agreement that free oxygen was present in much lower concentrations than that found today. Oxygen is a reactive substance, and would rapidly have formed compounds with the superficial materials of the Earth's crust. Haldane and Oparin accepted the view that not only is our present supply of oxygen replenished by plants, but that free oxygen has accumulated in our atmosphere as a result of its release from combination in the course of photosynthesis (*see* pages 44–5).

Oparin has attempted to outline a possible mode of transformation of organic chemicals, which accumulated in the oceans, into simple, localized systems from which the earliest organisms could have developed. He pointed out that, in water, organic chemicals do not necessarily remain uniformly dispersed, but may form layers and droplets. The formation of a particular kind of aggregate of fairly large molecules in water, so-called *coacervates*, had been studied by de Jong.[38] Under some conditions, droplets rich in chemical constituents may separate out from the 'solutions', and these droplets are surrounded by a tight 'skin' of water molecules (Fig. 20). They may join with each other, but do not mix with the surrounding water. These droplets have some features in common with living cells. Oparin argued that as organic compounds collected in the oceans, coacervates could have formed, and the constitution of these would have varied. Among the kinds formed, some would have been better able to persist than others. At this early stage, selective processes would have been at work, as the less stable droplets would be eliminated and a 'population' of stable

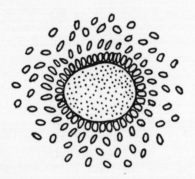

Fig. 20. Water molecules forming a 'skin' around an organic droplet, as in a coacervate. Large stippled oval = organic droplet. Small ovals = water molecules.

droplets built up. Oparin and his colleagues have studied the behaviour of coacervates made in the laboratory, and have shown that it is possible to incorporate enzymes in them.[37] If living things were formed in solutions of mixed chemicals, ways of bringing together the necessary molecules must have existed, and the coacervate theory, backed by some experimental evidence, provides one possible explanation.

The notion of selection of progressively more stable droplets is a natural 'backward' extension of Darwin's theory of natural selection among higher organisms. It seems almost self-evident that selective processes must have been operative from the earliest stages of chemical evolution. In any particular set of conditions, some materials or systems will be able to exist, and others will be eliminated. Natural selection is not some magical process imposed from without, but an expression of the complicated interactions which take place in nature. In the course of this evolutionary process, as Oparin[39] has pointed out, intermediate forms linking inanimate and animate systems might have been swept away, and this may be why we are now so keenly aware of a 'gulf separating organic from inorganic nature'.

In a more recent article, Haldane[40] has given a useful classification of theories of the origin of life, which may be summarized as follows:

1. Life has no origin. Matter and life have always existed.
2. Life originated on our planet by a supernatural event.
3. Life originated from ordinary chemical reactions by a slow evolutionary process.
4. Life originated as the result of a very 'improbable' event, which however was almost certain to happen given sufficient time, and sufficient matter of suitable composition in a suitable state.

We have already given some attention to the first two of these, and it is 3. and 4. which mainly concern us now. Haldane remarked that the theories grade into each other, but that he has stated them in extreme forms. It is probably true to say that the theories of group 3. are steadily gaining ground among biochemists. In 1954, Haldane was inclined to give some weight to 4., as he thought that the emergence of a workable cell might have demanded a statistically rather improbable set of conditions. If we imagine a number of similar planets, like the Earth, life would appear on all of them after roughly the same time if possibility 3. is true. If, however, one stage in the production of living things is highly 'improbable', there might be large differences in the time of appearance of organisms on the individual planets.

The Origins of Organic Chemicals. The theories we have so far considered postulate the production of organic chemicals under the influence of ultra-violet radiations, and the work of Baly gave some support to this view. In experiments of this kind, it is important to exclude any present-day organisms which might contaminate the mixture of simple chemicals used and, by their activities, produce changes which could be mistakenly attributed to light. More recent experimental work, in both the

U.S.A. and the U.S.S.R., has confirmed the possibility of trans-formations by ultra-violet radiations, and some other ways in which organic compounds can be produced have been discovered.

Oparin[2] has summarized the available work on the action of ultra-violet radiations. Molecules such as those of water, ammonia and hydrocarbons are split to give highly reactive chemical groups, or *radicals*, which can then react with each other or with other materials to produce new compounds.

Another source of energy for chemical reactions in the primitive atmosphere would have been electrical discharges, including lightning and corona discharges from pointed objects. Miller[41, 42] working in Urey's laboratory, was able to show that organic chemicals could be formed in artificial gas mixtures subjected to electrical discharges for about a week. Several different forms of apparatus were constructed for the experiments, and both spark and silent discharges were used. The gas mixture contained methane, ammonia, water vapour and hydrogen. At the conclusion of the experiments, several amino-acids had been formed, and numerous other organic chemicals. These substances were not produced if free oxygen was added to the mixture. Different gas mixtures were later investigated by Ableson,[43] who found that amino-acids were still produced if ammonia were replaced by nitrogen and methane by carbon dioxide or carbon monoxide (CO). Ableson also confirmed Miller's work. Further experiments along similar lines have been reported by Pavlovskaya and Pasynskii,[44] who have suggested that carbon monoxide might have been an important atmospheric constituent at the time of formation of amino-acids, and that free hydrogen was not essential.

Beta-Particle Bombardment. We have mentioned earlier that 'beta-rays' are streams of electrons. Hasselstrom[45] and his colleagues have studied the effects of bombarding a solution of ammonium acetate with beta-rays. The solutions were sealed in polythene bags and bombarded by electrons in a 2 million volt electron accelerator. This treatment resulted in the formation of two amino-acids, glycine and aspartic acids, and a third unidentified amino-acid. The investigators think it likely that the beta-rays decompose the water and ammonia by knocking out hydrogen atoms. The remaining groups or radicals then react with the ammonium acetate to produce amino-acids.

Gamma-radiation. Another recent investigation has demonstrated the production of organic compounds, including glycine, by exposure of ammonium carbonate to gamma-rays. Ammonium carbonate was sealed in glass tubes and subjected to gamma-ray bombardment from radioactive cobalt. Examination after fifteen days showed that some organic compounds had been formed. It is probable that enough radioactive ores were present on the primitive earth to permit reactions of this sort, and Paschke[46] and his colleagues have suggested that gamma radiation from terrestrial sources might have been more important than sunlight or electrical discharges for the production of organic chemicals.

Alpha-particles. An alpha-particle, it will be remembered, consists of two neutrons and two protons. Several instances have been reported of the formation of organic compounds from carbon dioxide and other substances under bombardment by alpha-particles. In 1926, Lind and Bardwell[47] were able to obtain resinous organic substances by alpha-particle irradiation of mixtures of carbon dioxide, carbon monoxide and hydrogen or methane. Sokolov[48] suggested that water in sedimentary formations would be split by alpha-rays to give hydrogen and oxygen. The oxygen would be removed by reaction with metals and any existing organic compounds, and the hydrogen might then lead to the production of methane from carbon dioxide. The methane so formed could form the starting point for the formation of hydrocarbons of higher molecular weight. Garrison[49] and his colleagues showed that organic compounds, including formic acid and formaldehyde, were formed when solutions of carbon dioxide in water were exposed to alpha-particles in a cyclotron.

It is clear that some reactions of this kind might have played a part in the formation and transformation of organic compounds on the primitive earth, as alpha-particles would have been emitted by radioactive materials of the crust. Oparin[2] suggested that the main rôle of sources of energy, including cosmic rays, alpha- and beta-particles, gamma-rays and electrical discharges, was the promotion of reactions among simple hydrocarbons which were, in his opinion, the most plentiful carbon compounds at that time. In support of his view that hydrocarbons were present, Oparin[2] quotes spectroscopic evidence from studies of stars, comets and planets which suggests that the production of hydrocarbons is widespread throughout the universe.

Organic 'Interstellar Smoke' Theory. Lederberg[50] has recently discussed the possibility that organic (carbonaceous) molecules might have been widespread in the universe. Among the elements, the lighter ones are by far the most prevalent, and in order of abundance carbon, oxygen and nitrogen follow hydrogen and helium. There is consequently reason to believe that the primitive condensation of atoms to form interstellar smoke would necessarily have led to the production of compounds of hydrogen, carbon, oxygen and nitrogen. It is therefore possible that vast quantities of organic molecules of great complexity were formed. In the prestellar smoke there would be greater likelihood of some molecules forming than others, and the energetics of the reactions would determine a form of chemical natural selection and a predominance of certain molecular 'species'. The spectra of comets, which contain evidence of the existence of compounds of carbon and hydrogen, are consistent with this view. Materials formed are carried into the Earth's atmosphere on meteorites. The intense heating of meteoric material on passage through the atmosphere may produce profound changes, but the examination of meteoric dust from the Moon, or collected by artificial satellites, might provide direct evidence of associated carbon-containing molecules.

The Primitive Atmosphere. Further Considerations. We have seen that Haldane[30] suggested that carbon was present in the primitive atmosphere as carbon dioxide, CO_2, whereas Oparin[2] favoured the presence of carbon in the chemically 'reduced' form; that is, combined with hydrogen as methane, CH_4. There is no final agreement on this point, and Vinogradov[51] has recently argued, on geological and geophysical grounds, that carbon was probably present as carbon monoxide, CO. He was led to this conclusion by a consideration of the composition of present-day volcanic gases, which contain water vapour, carbon dioxide, carbon monoxide and a number of other constituents, but methane is found, if at all, in only small amounts. Goldschmidt[52] stated that 'without doubt' the main carbon compound of the primitive atmosphere was carbon dioxide, a gas which has been discharged from the interior of the Earth during the whole of geological history. There is fairly general agreement that the primitive atmosphere contained little free oxygen.

The experimental work which has been mentioned shows that, whether carbon were present as CH_4 or CO_2, there were several possible means by which more complex carbon compounds might have been formed, so long as the concentration of free oxygen was low. Urey[53] has remarked that the biochemical arguments might be more conclusive evidence for the primitive atmosphere than any that can be derived from cosmochemical or geochemical studies, but that the latter confirm the biochemical conclusions.

The gas *ozone*, which filters off much of the short-wave ultraviolet solar radiation, is an *allotropic* form of oxygen. Whereas the ordinary oxygen molecule consists of two oxygen atoms combined together, O_2, the ozone molecule contains three oxygen atoms, O_3. Ozone can be formed by exposing oxygen to ultraviolet radiations, and to electrical discharges. In our atmosphere, it occurs mainly between 20 and 30 miles above the Earth. If all the ozone in the atmosphere could be collected and brought to sea level at 0° C., it would form a layer only about 3 mm. thick, but in spite of the seemingly small amount, it is an effective screen. A layer of ozone of this thickness is said to be roughly equivalent as an absorbing medium for ultra-violet radiations to a 500 m. thick layer of carbon dioxide, or 10 m. of clear water. It is possible that the view that the surface of the primitive earth was unscreened against solar ultra-violet radiation needs modification. Other products of gaseous dissociation might have exerted some screening effect, and very small quantities of ozone might have been formed from oxygen released by the splitting of water molecules by ultra-violet light, although, because of the low oxygen concentration, the amount of ozone would have been much less than at present. There was probably some grading of the wavelengths of radiations reaching progressively deeper layers of the atmosphere, and this might have affected the type of reaction possible at different levels.

Amino-Acid Mixtures and Protein Formation. There seems to be no difficulty in accounting for the formation of a variety of fairly complex carbon compounds on the primitive earth, and we may reasonably assume that similar stages in chemical evolution would have occurred on other similar planets in the universe. There is, too, the added possibility of acquisition of carbonaceous molecules from interstellar dust. At this stage, however, we have travelled only a small distance along the pathway to life, and it is now necessary to look for evidence that the necessary continuing increase in complexity of compounds could have occurred.

It has been explained that amino-acids may be regarded as the 'building blocks' of the much more complicated proteins. Proteins have been found in all living things which have so far been examined, and many investigators consider that they are an essential constituent of living organisms. Pirie[54], [27] has rightly warned that proteins may offer the most successful, rather than the only, way of living, and that the importance of present-day uniformity of the basic chemical composition of living organisms is often exaggerated. It is quite possible that organisms based on compounds other than proteins have existed, but have been replaced by those using proteins. There is, however, some recent evidence that protein-like substances might form in amino-acid mixtures in short periods of time, provided that certain conditions of proportions of different acids, and temperature, are met. Moreover, as has been pointed out by Fox,[55] in several experiments with somewhat different starting materials and conditions, organic compounds in the same rather narrow range of possibilities have resulted.

Thermal Synthesis of 'Proteinoids'. The investigations of Fox[56], [57] and his colleagues have revealed a mechanism for the formation of protein-like molecules (proteinoids) in amino-acid

58

mixtures. It was explained earlier that the amino-acid components of a protein molecule are linked by peptide bonds, and it can be seen from Fig. 21 that the formation of a peptide bond between amino-acids involves the loss of water. It seemed possible that peptide bonds might form in heated amino-acid mixtures if the temperature was high enough to drive off the water produced in the reaction. Earlier work on the heating of

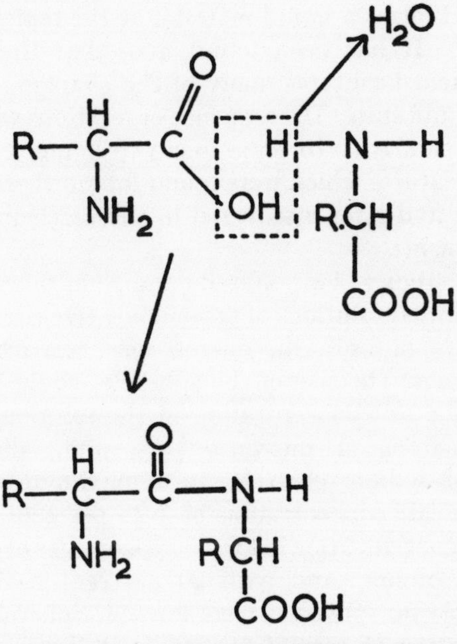

FIG. 21. Water removed in peptide bond formation.

amino-acid mixtures, however, gave little cause for hope, as only useless, tarry materials had been formed.

Fox and his collaborators were impressed by the fact that, of the twenty or so amino-acids found in proteins, two, known as glutamic acid and aspartic acid, were present in greater amounts than the others. These two acids made up about a quarter to a half of the protein molecules. It is further known that aspartic and glutamic acids play certain key rôles in biological processes. Harada and Fox therefore tried heating a mixture of amino-acids in which glutamic and aspartic acids were present in excess, and they found that after three hours heating at about 180° C. a protein-like material had been produced. In various experiments proteinoids with molecular weights ranging from 3000 to 10,000 were formed, and they contained some of each of the amino-acids of the original mixture.

Fox has pointed out that the reactions in heated amino-acid mixtures need not be solid reactions, because, when heated, glutamic acid forms a liquid material at the temperatures used (160–180° C.). It has been found, too, that the inclusion of phosphoric acid facilitates many of the changes, and this also provides a liquid state. The sequence of reactions which occurred bore a close similarity to some found in living organisms, and Fox quotes features which were found first in thermal synthesis experiments, and later discovered in the biochemical mechanisms of organisms.

In further studies, Fox, Harada and Kendrick[58] have shown that hot saturated solutions of proteinoids give rise on cooling to huge numbers of uniform, microscopic, relatively firm and elastic spherules. The size of the spherules could be influenced by varying the salt concentration in the solution, and ranged from 1·4 microns (1 micron = $\frac{1}{1000}$ mm.) diameter with 0·15 per cent sodium chloride, to a maximum of about 2·5 microns at a salt concentration of 1·25 per cent. Further increase in salt concentration led to decrease in size of the spherules produced on cooling, and with 20 per cent sodium chloride present, almost no spherules were formed. Spherules were produced by heating 15 mg. of proteinoid in 3 ml. of sea water, boiling for one minute, and allowing to cool to room temperature. The spherules retained their form for several weeks. These interesting observations might help towards a better understanding of ways in which primitive cells or cell-like bodies could have been formed from suitable starting solutions of organic compounds.

Possible Rôle of Clay and Other Minerals. Bernal[9, 18] has suggested that many crystalline substances, such as quartz and aluminium silicate clays, were probably present in the primitive oceans. It is known that organic molecules may become stuck, or 'adsorbed', to the surfaces of particles of this kind, so that clay and sand might have helped to bring together the simpler molecules which could then react more easily to form complicated compounds. In addition, concentration might have occurred in the spaces between particles, even without adsorption. It seems likely that the mineral particles did not act merely as passive traps, but also catalysed some reactions, but this possibility requires more thorough investigation in artificial systems in the laboratory. Bernal stresses the importance of a medium free from turbulence, in which the diffusion of small molecules would be restricted so that a considerable concentration could be built up. These conditions might have existed in mud beds, under water, on land or in regions alternately wet and dry, as in tidal estuaries. After larger molecules had been formed from small molecules, the need for mineral support diminished; the new large molecules would themselves perform the function for which the mineral particles were formerly necessary. The new molecules formed could be the starting point for the production of coacervates.

Mechanisms of this kind might have permitted the development of primitive organisms, a 'protoplankton', without the necessity for an organic 'soup' of the sort envisaged by Haldane and Oparin. It is possible that the presence of adsorbents, including clay, would have prevented the formation of soups of chemicals. Ableson, at the Oceanographic Congress in 1959, pointed out that the purely random reaction of organic molecules in watery solution tends to produce unusable, tar-like masses. It is therefore probable that mineral catalysts in some form were essential to the early stages of biopœsis, and that in this respect the original Haldane–Oparin theory needs modification. After synthesis of organic molecules in the primitive atmosphere and their passage to the oceans and moist regions of the Earth, the concentrating and directing influence of minerals probably influenced profoundly the course of chemical evolution.

Other Possibilities. Pringle[59, 60] has discussed the problem of the localization of chemicals into units from a rather different point of view. He is not greatly impressed by the Haldane–Oparin theory, believing that the inability of present-day organisms to make use of ultra-violet light as a source of energy can be used as an argument against the direct biological importance of these wavelengths in the past. He suggests that the main effects of ultra-violet radiations would have been in the upper layers of the atmosphere, splitting water molecules to give oxygen and hydrogen, and other molecules to give reactive chemical groups, or 'radicals'.

If the temperature of the primitive earth was higher than the present temperature, the water vapour content of the atmosphere would have been greater, so that although short-wave ultra-violet radiations would have penetrated farther into the atmosphere than they can today, they would have been absorbed to some extent by water. Pringle therefore suggested that the important factor producing chemical change at the surface, was a 'rain' of small amounts of oxygen and peroxides, coming from the upper atmosphere. These reacted with hydrocarbons which had been formed from metal carbides and water. The low-temperature oxidation of hydrocarbons under these conditions would have been by reactions proceeding in stages, chemical 'chain reactions'.

To account for the concentration of the compounds formed into restricted localities, Pringle makes use of a mathematical demonstration by Turing that certain types of initially homogeneous dynamic systems undergo a progressive change which leads to the appearance of spatial heterogeneity. For the occurrence of a true evolutionary process, there must be a mechanism which allows competition between units, so that the more efficient survive. Pringle points out that even in seemingly simple chemical reactions, there may be competing routes by which a reaction can proceed, and that in complex reaction mixtures there will be greater possibilities for diversity. There is, he claims, a place for a biological approach to the problems of some of these chemical reactions, based on an analogy with the dynamics of populations of living organisms. These interesting suggestions are based on rather complicated theories, and cannot be discussed in more detail here.

Asymmetric Synthesis. In the section on proteins it was explained that certain optical isomers, the L-amino acids, predominate in living organisms, and it is necessary to try to account for this. There are, it now seems, several mechanisms which might have given rise to optically active carbon compounds on the Earth in the pre-biological era (see Oparin[2]), including the action of circularly polarized light on mixtures of simple chemicals, and reactions at the surfaces of optically active crystals, such as quartz. There is no need to invoke some peculiar 'vital force' which selected the L- rather than the D-isomers for incorporation in organisms, as several possible alternative theories can be formulated.

One possible mechanism is postulated in the *critical complex theory* of Eyring and Johnson.[61] According to these authors, a critical phase in chemical evolution might have been reached with the formation of a 'template', probably a ribonucleic acid molecule of greater length and configurational perfection than had previously occurred. At this instant, the world 'went critical', and replication of this template and the crude enzymes concerned in its formation took place within a shorter time than their own 'life spans'. This shut the door on competitors with different optical activity, and biological evolution began. The rates of reactions involved in a process of this kind have been calculated, and it seems possible that in concentrated solutions of the necessary starting materials, optical activity might arise in a few days.

Pirie[54] has suggested that the selection of the L-isomers might have occurred at a later stage. If, initially, two separate lines of organisms, one type using the D-isomers and the other L-isomers, were produced, and if both types shared the need for some common raw materials, one type may have competed more successfully for the materials and so have ousted the other. This could have occurred in the 1,000,000,000 years or so preceding the start of the fossil record. On this view, it is unnecessary to postulate pre-biological selection of one isomer.

The 'interstellar smoke' theory of the origin of organic molecules offers another possible solution of the problem of asymmetry. It has been found that light traversing interstellar material is polarized. The photochemical action of polarized light can favour the formation of one type of isomer, so that it is possible that important optically active biochemical precursor molecules were formed at an early stage in chemical evolution. These, incorporated in or arriving on suitable planets might set the bias in favour of one type of molecule.

Interplanetary travel may make it possible, in the not too distant future, to study organisms on Mars or Venus, if such

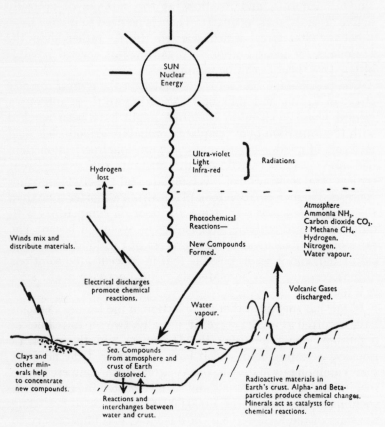

FIG. 22.   The Primitive Earth as a Chemical Factory.

exist. It will be of great interest to determine whether or not the same optical isomers predominate as on the Earth. A predominance of D-isomers would be of particular significance, as it would suggest that the predominance of L-isomers in terrestrial organisms is a chance phenomenon. If life on another planet is associated with L-isomers, further conclusions will not be possible, as with only two similar examples the selection of L-isomers might still be random. It may, of course, become possible to reproduce the early stages of biopœsis in terrestrial laboratories, and solve the problem that way. Keosian[62] has suggested that it is possible, though improbable, that living organisms can be formed only with L-isomers predominating, for some reason we do not yet know. If that were so, the 'choice' would have been necessary, in the sense that it was the only possible sequence of events.

Conclusion

A real beginning has been made in the experimental approach to the problem of transition of matter from inorganic to organic states, from pre-biological to biological modes of organization. It is becoming apparent that there are many possible ways in which organic compounds could have been formed, and in different environments one or another method might have predominated. The accumulating evidence seems rather to favour the view that the production of living from non-living matter may be expected to follow various strictly determined reaction sequences, although the set of sequences appropriate to one planetary environment might differ in detail from that which would occur under slightly different conditions. The emergence of 'life' in certain places in the universe may be as necessary a feature of the behaviour of matter as, for example, the neutralization of an acid by an alkali, although tremendously more complicated.

III

MYTHS OR MEN?

Before dealing with our neighbour worlds in more detail, in an attempt to decide whether any of them can support life, it is worth saying a little about past ideas on the subject. Speculations have not been lacking, though it is only recently that these speculations have been backed by adequate scientific knowledge.

Ancient Ideas. The ancients knew that the Earth is a globe; this was the case also for the Moon, the planets and possibly the stars. There seemed to be a host of heavenly bodies, and why should not some, at least, be inhabited? A philosopher of classical Greece had no means of analyzing the atmosphere of a planet, or even of knowing for certain whether such an atmosphere existed at all; he could only guess as to the temperature, the amount of moisture, and the surface conditions generally. Neither had he any real knowledge about the sizes of the planets, or their distances from us.

The most obvious dwelling-place for 'other men' seemed to be the Moon, which was regarded as cool and earthy. Anaxagoras wrote that 'it has an admixture of cold and of earth. It has a surface in some places lofty, in others hollow.' This is by no means a bad description, but the earliest complete book devoted to possible lunar life did not come until about A.D. 70. This was Plutarch's *De Facie in Orbe Lunæ*, to which reference has already been made.

Plutarch's book contains some science and a great deal of imagination. Though he agreed with Anaxagoras that the Moon is a second Earth, with mountains, valleys and ravines scattered over its surface, he rejected the idea of human inhabitants, and replaced them with demons. The second part of the essay is in dialogue form, and describes the wanderings of departed souls as they glide between Earth and Moon.

It is not clear how seriously Plutarch himself took these speculations, but the next book to contain an account of lunar life, written by Lucian of Samosata half a century later, was pure satire. It was called the *True History*, because, according to the author himself, it was made up of nothing but lies from beginning to end. It describes how a party of adventurers sailing through the Pillars of Hercules (the Strait of Gibraltar) is caught in a waterspout, and whirled up to the Moon. The travellers arrive in time to take part in a full-scale interplanetary war. The King of the Moon has quarrelled with the King of the Sun as to who should have prior claim in the colonization of Venus, and the two armies fight with such allies as cabbagefowls, horse-griffins, sky-crows and centaurs . . .

Tales of the Seventeenth Century. Lucian's book is well worth reading, but in the present context it would be out of place to consider it further. Neither can we do much more than mention the various other stories produced later, such as Johannes Kepler's famous *Somnium*, published in 1634. Kepler was the great mathematician who first proved conclusively that the planets move round the Sun in elliptical orbits, but he was also a mystic, and his novel is a medley of proper seventeenth-century science together with supernatural ideas. The hero of the story—Duracotus, a young Icelander—travels to the Moon with the help of his mother Fiolxhilda, who is an accomplished witch. On arrival, he finds a strange world indeed. 'The moon-dwellers are furry beings, indeed fur makes up the larger part of their bodies, which are spongy, puffy and porous. If a moon-being is caught unawares by the great heat of the day, his fur is singed and becomes hard and brittle so that in the evening it drops off. . . . Most moon-dwellers have serpentine bodies and enjoy lying in the moderate heat of the morning or evening sun . . . all over the Moon lie great masses of acorns. The scales of these cones are scorched by the Sun during the day. Then, in the evening, the cones open and new moon-dwellers are born.'

Equally entertaining, and much more pleasant, was *The Man in the Moone*, written by the Bishop of Hereford, Francis

Godwin, and published posthumously in 1638. The hero, Domingo Gonzales, travels to the Moon in a raft towed by gansas (wild geese), and encounters all manner of wonders. However, Godwin certainly did not intend his book to be anything more than a story. This also applies to many of the other books on the subject produced during the seventeenth and eighteenth centuries.

However, ideas were changing. The true status of the Earth had been realized; instead of being of fundamental importance, it was a very junior body in the universe as a whole. Many astronomers of justly wide repute came to believe that some of the planets, if not all, must be inhabited. The most celebrated of these men was William Herschel.

Development of Scientific Thought. As we have seen, Herschel may be regarded as the greatest pioneer in the field of stellar astronomy. He was a superb observer, and also the best telescope-maker of his day; his largest reflector, with a focal length of 40 feet, remained unequalled until the erection of Lord Rosse's 72-inch in 1845. Herschel also served as the first president of the Royal Astronomical Society, and received virtually all the honours that the scientific world could bestow.

In many ways Herschel was far in advance of his time, but he held some ideas which were curiously extreme. He thought that the habitability of the Moon was 'an absolute certainty', and he was equally convinced that there were intelligent beings not only on the planets, but also inside the Sun, which he believed to have a hot surface covering a cool, temperate region.

Herschel made no secret of these opinions. By no means all his contemporaries agreed with him, but there was no suggestion that he would be laughed at. His contemporary Johann Schröter, first of the great lunar observers, believed that certain 'changes' on the Moon indicated vital activity there, while in the mid-nineteenth century the German astronomer Franz Gruithuisen announced the discovery of a true lunar city, with 'dark gigantic ramparts'.

In the popular view, too, the existence of men on the Moon and planets seemed more than likely. In 1835, for instance, many readers of the *New York Sun* were deceived by an elaborate hoax, in which the paper reported that Sir John Herschel (William Herschel's son), working at the Cape of Good Hope, had discovered life-forms on the Moon ranging from horned sheep to grey pelicans, bat-men, and even 'a strange amphibious creature of a spherical form, which rolled with great velocity across the pebbly beach'. The hoax was exposed before long, but it had a wide circulation.

The success of the hoax, combined with the views of men such as William Herschel and Schröter, is not so surprising as it may sound. At that time the hostile nature of the Moon and most of the planets was by no means generally appreciated, even by astronomers. It was reasonable enough to assume that advanced life would develop on any suitable world, and it was only when scientific progress revealed the unsuitability of the bodies of the Solar System that serious doubts began to creep in.

For instance, it became clear that the Moon's atmosphere, far from being dense and breathable—as Schröter, for instance, had believed—is so tenuous that it can hardly support any form of life, and is certainly useless so far as men or animals are concerned. Even when the Moon had been crossed off the list, however, Mars remained; Lowell's book advocating the hypothesis of artificial canals was published as recently as 1906, and it was only when the Martian atmosphere could be properly analyzed that the artificial-canal theory had to be abandoned.

Scientific opinion changed accordingly, and the pendulum swung right over.

We now know that of all the worlds in the Solar System, only the Earth has an atmosphere which could be breathed by men such as ourselves, and it is therefore safe to reject terrestrial-type Selenites and Martians. Yet we must avoid being dogmatic. We have a great advantage over our predecessors, since we have the equipment to give us positive information about other planets; where Herschel and Schröter could only guess, we are in a position to give a balanced judgement. If life exists beyond the Earth, what form is it likely to take—and where is it likely to be found?

That is the state of the problem today.

IV

THE MOON

Of all the bodies in the sky, the Moon can be studied in the most detail. There are two reasons for this. First, it is extremely close; its average distance from the Earth is less than a quarter of a million miles. Secondly, it is virtually devoid of atmosphere, so that there is nothing to obscure its surface features.

General Data. The Moon has a diameter of 2160 miles. It is therefore smaller (and also less massive) than any of the planets, but it appears to be too large for a normal satellite, since its mass is $\frac{1}{81}$ of that of the Earth. Several other known satellites are larger than the Moon, but are nevertheless much less massive relative to their primaries. The old idea that the Moon broke away from the Earth, leaving the depression now filled by the Pacific Ocean, has been abandoned; it is generally agreed that the Moon was formed in the same manner as the Earth itself, and at the same epoch. On the whole, it is best to regard the Earth-Moon system as a double planet rather than as a planet and a satellite.

The Moon is less dense than the Earth. Its specific gravity is 3·34, only 0·6 that of our world; the surface gravity also is lower, and has been calculated at 0·16 of that of the Earth. It will be clear that the mean density of the Moon is not very different from that of the terrestrial surface rocks, and accordingly it has been suggested that the Moon has no core similar to that of the Earth. Support for this idea has been provided by the fact that measures made in 1959 with the first two Russian-launched moon probes (Luniks I and II) indicate that the lunar magnetic field is weak—so weak, indeed, that it cannot at present be measured. A body lacking a substantial terrestrial-type core would be expected to lack a powerful magnetic field, so that the Russian results are not surprising.[1]

Surface Features. Even a moderate telescope reveals great detail on the Moon. There are the large dark plains known as 'seas'; the mountains and peaks; the features known variously as clefts, rills or rilles; swellings or domes, and of course the numerous walled circular formations which are always termed craters. These craters range in size from the immense formation Bailly, almost 180 miles in diameter, down to tiny pits. Of the various lunar maps produced during the last hundred years, special mention should be made of that produced by H. P. Wilkins.[2] A photographic atlas has also been produced by G. P. Kuiper and his colleagues in the United States,[3] and is a valuable reference source, though unfortunately the photographs are of very variable quality.

The problem of the origin of the lunar craters has caused endless discussion, and is still not settled. Some authorities believe the craters to be meteoric, produced by impacts of bodies from space. This theory has been described in detail by R. B. Baldwin,[4] and has received wide support. However, the non-random distribution of the craters, together with certain other special features, leads to the suggestion that the craters are basically volcanic, though the large lunar formations are by no means similar to terrestrial volcanoes such as Vesuvius. Moore[5] has proposed a tentative 'uplift and subsidence' theory to account for the major craters and the domes. It is worth noting that many domes and rounded hills are crowned by summit pits, so that they really do resemble Earth-type volcanoes. Some of these have been catalogued by Moore and Cattermole.[6] More recently, Kuiper has also drawn attention to 13 of the objects contained in the earlier lists.[7]

Surface Changes? The lunar surface seems to be almost changeless. There is of course the classic case of the formation Linné, which was described before 1843 as a well-marked crater, and since 1866 as a tiny pit surrounded by a whitish nimbus; but the evidence in favour of alteration is generally thought to be inconclusive. However, on November 3rd, 1958, the Russian astronomer N. A. Kozyrev, working with the 50-inch reflector at the Crimean Astrophysical Observatory, observed an outbreak inside the large crater Alphonsus, and was able to take spectrograms which revealed gaseous emission. There can be no doubt as to the reality of this disturbance.[8]

We must be wary of drawing too close an analogy with a terrestrial volcanic outbreak. S. Miyamoto[9] has drawn attention to the possibility that gases trapped below the crust may be released when the surface is fractured in any way, and this may be a better explanation, though proof is lacking. It seems, however, that the older reports of 'obscurations' in or near various craters cannot be dismissed as summarily as many authorities tended to do before Kozyrev's observation. The balance of evidence now indicates that the Moon is not completely inert.

Nature of the Lunar Surface. The question of the genesis of the lunar craters is important in many ways—not least because it must affect our views as to the nature of the surface. Local colour is virtually absent from the Moon, and the general impression is of a surface overlaid with a layer of ash or dust. This may or may not be correct, but mention must be made of a theory due to T. Gold,[10] according to which the seas or *maria* are covered with a dusty layer kilometres deep. Gold paints a pessimistic picture from the astronomical viewpoint, since he has maintained that 'space-travellers of the future will simply sink into the dust'.

There are various objections to this hypothesis, both on observational and on theoretical grounds, and it seems more likely that any ashy or dusty layer is of slight depth. One way of tackling the problem is by temperature measurements made conventionally, by use of the thermocouple, and at radio wavelengths.

The Moon's virtual lack of atmosphere means that the variations in temperature between day and night are very great judged by terrestrial standards. On the lunar equator, the range is between about $+216°$ Fahrenheit and $-250°$ Fahrenheit, as measured by E. Pettit and S. B. Nicholson[11] and others. There is little doubt as to the validity of these figures. However, measures made at radio wavelengths yield different results. In 1949, J. H. Piddington and H. C. Minnett[12] experimented at a wavelength of 1·25 cm., and found a much smaller range, with maximum temperature occurring well after full moon. These investigations related to a layer below the actual crust, and other experiments, such as those at 3·2 cm. by B. Troitsky and M. Zelinskaya;[13] 10 cm. by K. Akabane[14] and J. E. Gibson[15] confirm that the temperature range diminishes with increasing depth. This is naturally to be expected. The results have been used by J. C. Jaeger and A. F. Harper[16] to suggest a model according to which there is a thin dusty or ashy layer, perhaps a few millimetres thick, overlaying solid volcanic rock.

Great attention to this problem has been paid by Russian astronomers.[17] According to photometric, spectral and polarization tests carried out at Kharkov Observatory, under the supervision of N. Barabashov,[18] the surface is covered by a layer of disintegrated tufa-like rock, with grains varying in size from 3 to 10 mm. It is considered that this layer of crushed material is less than 5 cm. deep, and is unlikely to provide a hazard for future space-travellers.

To sum up, then, it is fair to say that although Gold's hypothesis of very deep dust-drifts has not been disproved, it must be regarded as rather improbable.

Atmosphere. In the present context, little more need be said about the existence or non-existence of a lunar atmosphere. There are any number of reasons for believing that any atmosphere must be highly rarefied; even the figure of $\frac{1}{10,000}$ of that of the Earth's atmosphere at sea-level, given by Y. N. Lipski in 1949 following polarimetric studies,[19] seems to be a great overestimate. The best results so far have been obtained by radio measures. Sometimes the Moon passes in front of, and occults, a radio source—the Crab Nebula in Taurus being one such source —and any lunar atmosphere might be expected to produce appreciable refraction effects. In 1954, Kuiper[20] gave a value for the lunar atmosphere of 10^{-13}, and similar investigations were made two years later by astronomers at Cambridge, when the Crab Nebula was occulted on January 24, 1956.[21] Polarization studies by A. Dollfus, at the high-altitude Pic du Midi

Observatory[22] have given negative results, but the validity of this method has been questioned by V. A. Firsoff,[23] and it will be obvious that the observations are extremely delicate.

If a very tenuous atmosphere exists, as seems probable, it may consist of gases released by radioactive processes in the lunar rocks; these gases may not be permanently retained by the Moon.

The Averted Side of the Moon. In this connection, it is worth referring to an old theory due to the nineteenth-century Danish astronomer Hansen, according to which the centre of gravity of the Moon was not coincident with the centre of figure, so that all the air and water had been drawn round to the far side. It will be remembered that 41 per cent of the Moon is permanently averted from the Earth, since the period taken for the Moon to turn once on its axis is the same as the orbital period (27 days 7 hours 43 minutes).

Hansen's theory was unsound, and met with little support even at the time when it was advanced. Recently, the flight of the Russian vehicle Lunik III, in October 1959, has given some positive information as to the Moon's far side. As was confidently expected, the newly-examined regions prove to be essentially similar to the old. There are fewer maria, but the Lunik pictures show a surface of the familiar type—equally barren and equally hostile. Of course, day and night conditions, as well as temperatures, are the same on the Moon's far side as on the side which we can see from Earth.

Pickering's Theories. No twentieth-century astronomer would ever maintain that advanced life-forms may exist on the Moon. However, there have been suggestions that primitive plant life may linger on there.

One of the main protagonists of this theory was W. H. Pickering, an American astronomer of considerable experience and repute. Up to his death in 1938, Pickering still believed in the existence of living matter in certain selected areas, such as the crater Eratosthenes. He based his views on the observation of dark areas which changed during the course of each lunation, and which he regarded as indicative of spreading plants—or even swarms of insects. Pickering's papers[24] tend to make rather strange reading today, but it is true that the patches inside Eratosthenes and a few other craters, such as Alphonsus and Endymion, are extremely interesting objects.

Moore has carried out a long study of Eratosthenes, and has come to the conclusion that the patches do not in fact spread and change as Pickering believed; it is thought more probable that the apparent variations can be explained much more convincingly as the result of the ever-changing angle of illumination from which we view them. There seems to be no valid reason to attribute them to plants.

Equally interesting are the curious dark streaks or radial bands seen in some craters. The most famous example is Aristarchus, the most brilliant object on the Moon—indeed, no less an authority than Herschel once mistook it for an active volcano when he saw it on the 'dark' side, illuminated by earthshine. Even a 3-in. refractor will show two of the radial bands, and larger instruments increase the total to at least six. Other, smaller craters show similar features. However, the suggestion that these too might be due to primitive plant life, supported by gases released from cracks in the surface under the influence of the Sun's heat, seems to be incompatible with modern results.

Is life possible under present lunar conditions? The picture which has been outlined does not suggest that there is a strong possibility of the first lunar explorers finding indigenous living things. The absence of water, if complete, would rule out the existence of active, functioning organisms of the type we know. Any organisms which existed on the lunar surface would have to be protected in some way against the impact of the full spectrum of solar radiation, as well as cosmic rays, unmodified by their passage through the extremely tenuous lunar atmosphere. Moreover, much of the surface is subjected to extremes of temperature variation in the course of the lunar day and night.

There are some places, however, where conditions might be less hostile, as for instance the entrances of caverns and portions of the floors of certain craters, such as Newton. In these localities, direct sunlight may never penetrate, but there may be diffuse illumination by light scattered from rocks or surface dust. The main difficulty is to imagine how any organisms at the lunar surface could obtain and retain water. Any water reaching the surface would almost instantaneously, even explosively, vaporize, because the atmospheric pressure is almost zero. At an atmospheric pressure of 4·58 mm. of mercury water 'boils' at 0° C., and liquid water cannot exist at lower pressures. It is, in any case, probable that most if not all of the Moon's water is held chemically combined as water of crystallization in rocks.

We will probably be correct if we conclude that conditions at the lunar surface are in many ways beyond the limits of biological adaptation. Many micro-organisms can, under suitable conditions, remain in dormant, dried or frozen states for long periods of time, even for many years.[25] The spores of some of our hardier bacteria might be able to survive on the Moon if sheltered from damaging solar ultra-violet and X- radiations, but in the absence of water and suitable nutrients—nitrogen and carbon compounds—they could not multiply. The remote possibility of 'subterranean' life on airless worlds is further discussed in Chapter VII.

We have seen that the primitive atmosphere of the Earth probably contained some ammonia, carbon dioxide, water and perhaps methane, and that under the influence of solar radiations various organic chemicals were formed from these. The Moon may once have had a similar atmosphere, its present virtually 'airless' state resulting from readier loss of gases because of the much lower lunar escape velocity. It is possible, then, that a variety of organic chemicals may be found on the Moon, perhaps below the surface layer, and C. Sagan has recently argued the case for this.[26] In the course of the evolution of living matter on the Earth, modifications of the atmosphere have helped to make possible the emergence of more complex forms with more efficient metabolic patterns; but on a body such as the Moon, which was losing its atmosphere fairly rapidly, the course of evolution might have stopped at a stage which we would consider pre-biological. It may be, therefore, that organic chemicals, capable of supporting the growth of micro-organisms, exist in the lunar surface.

Although it is most unlikely, if not impossible, that there are indigenous lunar organisms, the implantation of terrestrial micro-organisms at some depth in the Moon's surface might in some cases be followed by multiplication where water seepage and release of gases from deeper regions was occurring. Only beneath the surface, under some pressure, could liquid water exist, if any free water remains on the Moon.

To sum up, we may be sure that nearly all terrestrial organisms would find the Moon a hostile world. If, in the past, the Moon had an appreciable atmosphere, there is a very remote chance that specially adapted forms of living things might persist in restricted localities. There is, however, a distinct possibility that the surface layer may hide the products of a pre-biological type of chemical evolution which took place on the Moon ages ago, and the materials found there might give us useful clues as to the nature of terrestrial processes of the distant past. It is for this reason that biologists are anxious to avoid contamination of the lunar surface with terrestrial micro-organisms which might be able to persist, or even just possibly grow, and so modify a valuable record of chemical history.

A most interesting suggestion has recently been made by J. J. Gilvarry.[27] Gilvarry supposes that in past ages the Moon had a considerable hydrosphere, which lasted for perhaps 10^9 years, and had a maximum depth of in the region of 1 km. so that it drowned all the lowlands and encroached upon the highlands; the maria floors were formed by sediments deposited by the water in the course of its dissipation, so that the rocks of the maria floors are sedimentary in origin. It is assumed that the reason for the dark colour of the maria lies in the fact that a small amount of organic carbon in a sediment is sufficient to yield a dark rock of low reflectivity, so that a primitive form of life existed in the lunar hydrosphere. Gilvarry states that there is a positive clue that the seas of the Moon contained life; as the hydrosphere decreased, the dark coloration in Mare Imbrium and other seas of similar type tended to recede from the bases of encircling mountains; this is evident, for instance, in the Mare Nectaris, where the dark material has receded about 100 km. from the ring defined by the arc of the Altai Mountains. It is characteristic of living matter to follow the retreat of its habitat in this manner.

Gilvarry's hypothesis is highly speculative, and it is probably true to say that few authorities will be inclined to accept the former existence of an extensive hydrosphere. However, positive proof or disproof will be difficult to obtain until direct exploration of the lunar surface can be carried out.

Survival on the Moon. Direct contact with the Moon was established in September 1959, when the Russian vehicle Lunik II landed on the surface. Before long it will certainly be possible to send instrumented probes, and bring them down gently enough to avoid damaging them, so that we will be provided with a full-scale lunar transmitting station.

Few astronomers now doubt that men will land on the Moon before the end of the present century, but the problems of survival will be severe. By landing away from the equatorial regions it will be possible to avoid the intense daytime heat, but there is no evading the cold of night. Full protection must also be afforded against cosmic and ultra-violet radiation, and possibly against meteoric bombardment, since it now seems that the lunar atmosphere is too tenuous to act as an efficient screen. Whether the much-publicized 'lunar base' in the form of a plastic dome, inflated by the pressure of air inside it, will be practicable remains to be decided. On the credit side, medical research indicates that the reduced gravity will present no problems, and that human explorers will easily adapt themselves to it.

All this lies in the future. Meanwhile, it is clear that the Moon, hostile though it may be, is a fascinating world—and a world which may yet hold many surprises in store for us.

V

MARS

In some ways Mars is the most earthlike of our neighbour planets. Moreover it is closer than any other natural body in the sky apart from the Moon and Venus, and its relatively thin atmosphere results in its surface features appearing clear-cut. It is smaller and less massive than the Earth, as will be seen from the following table:

Data for Mars

Distance from the Sun:	max. 154,500,000 miles
	mean 141,500,000 ,,
	min. 128,500,000 ,,
Orbital eccentricity:	0·0093
Sidereal period:	687 days
Axial rotation period:	24 h. 37 m.
Diameter:	4200 miles
Mass, Earth = 1:	0·11
Specific gravity:	4·0
Surface gravity, Earth = 1:	0·38
Escape velocity:	3·1 miles per second

Atmosphere. The value of the escape velocity suggests that Mars should be able to retain an appreciable atmosphere. This is in fact the case. The barometric pressure on the Martian surface is given by Dollfus[1] as 83 millibars, which is similar to that experienced in the terrestrial atmosphere at an altitude of 11 miles above the ground. In fact, the Martian surface pressure is much less than that which prevails on the top of Mount Everest.

The precise composition of the Martian mantle is still not certainly known; the figures given in 1954 by G. de Vaucouleurs[2] are probably the best available. De Vaucouleurs maintains that 98·5 per cent of the atmosphere is due to nitrogen, about 1·2 per cent to argon, 0·25 per cent to carbon dioxide, and less than 0·1 per cent to oxygen.

This composition seems less encouraging than might have been hoped. The atmosphere is not of the kind which may be expected to support advanced life-forms. Water-vapour, too, is extremely scarce. Yet it would be unwise to conclude that this analysis is wholly reliable; the spectroscopic observations are delicate, and may be subject to considerable errors.

Clouds and Climate. 'Clouds' are often observed. Some, the 'blue clouds', may be due to high-altitude ice crystals, analogous to our cirrus. There are lower-level 'white clouds', which, unlike the former, are visible in moderate telescopes, and may become striking. Finally there are the 'yellow clouds', which may at times blot out much of the disk. The great yellow cloud of 1911, studied by E. M. Antoniadi at the Meudon Observatory, covered a large part of the southern hemisphere, and persisted for many weeks.[3] Various theories have been advanced to explain these yellow clouds. E. J. Öpik[4] believes them to be due to minor planets striking Mars and stirring up dust-clouds; this seems however to be far-fetched, and it is much more probable that the dust-clouds are whipped up from the surface by winds.[5] Generally speaking, wind-speeds on Mars are gentle by terrestrial standards, but the forces inside a weather system of the cyclone type might well be sufficient to produce the effects observed.

At any rate, rainfall on Mars does not occur; the last showers there must have taken place many ages ago. The whole planet is desperately short of moisture, and the dryness of the atmosphere is alone sufficient to show that oceans cannot exist there.

Moisture is not entirely absent. Among the most striking features of Mars are the polar caps, whitish areas covering the poles and which show seasonal changes. During winter of the hemisphere concerned, the cap may be very extensive, but shrinks rapidly during the spring, and by summer becomes very small; indeed, the southern cap has been known to vanish entirely. Spectroscopic work by G. Kuiper[6] has shown that they are due to H_2O frost at low temperature, and not, as had been previously suggested, to solid carbon dioxide. No close comparison should, however, be drawn with the thick ice-caps which cover the Arctic and Antarctic regions of our own world. De Vaucouleurs[7] has given sound reasons for supposing that the

Martian caps are less than 6 inches deep, and probably less than 3 inches. When they shrink with the arrival of warmer weather, they may sublime rather than melt—that is to say, pass directly from the solid to the gaseous state.

A new interpretation of Martian phenomena has recently been proposed by Kiess *et al.*,[8] who suggest that the atmosphere may contain several different oxides of nitrogen. The polar caps, they believe, consist of deposits of solid nitrogen tetroxide. At polar temperatures above $-40°$ C. the polar caps will be chalky white, tinged with the yellow of nitrogen dioxide. At higher temperatures, the yellowish colour will deepen and become brownish, but at lower temperatures a greenish-blue hue may be produced. The reddish colour of the planet and its albedo follow from the optical properties of nitrogen peroxide. The dark-coloured fringe seen during the retreat of the polar caps could be produced by liquid nitrogen tetroxide, with the trioxide and dioxide in solution, and by combination of the oxides with surface minerals. The various atmospheric clouds can also be accounted for, but the surface phenomena seen would indicate that the atmospheric pressure is about 140 mm. mercury, instead of 70 mm., the generally accepted value. This ingenious unified theory of Martian phenomena, which is not contradicted by available spectroscopic findings, would, if proved, radically alter our conception of the suitability of Mars for life; it would be doubtful if any terrestrial organisms could survive there, for free water is presumed to be absent, and the gases are poisonous to known organisms. Mars would simply be 'the locale of a gigantic photochemical nitrogen-fixation process'. The theory is, as yet, far from being established, and requires further investigation.

The thin, dry atmosphere is by no means efficient at retaining the daytime warmth. At noon on the equator, the temperature may rise to almost 80° Fahrenheit, but at midnight it must drop to well below $-100°$ Fahrenheit. Polar nights are even colder. Since the rotation period of Mars is not much longer than our own, the changes in temperature there are comparatively rapid.

The climate is influenced by the fact that high mountain ranges seem to be absent. Appreciable differences in level doubtless occur, but there are no chains of peaks comparable with the Himalayas or even the Alps of the Earth. Dollfus has calculated[9] that there may be plateaux in the polar regions of up to 3000 feet, but this is very arbitrary.

Dark Areas. The famous dark patches on Mars, first seen by Christiaan Huygens as long ago as 1659, have been adequately mapped. Some, such as the Syrtis Major and Sinus Sabæus, may be seen with small telescopes when Mars is well placed; others are less evident. Their outlines appear to be more or less permanent, and they show seasonal changes, since during the shrinking of the polar cap there seems to be a 'wave of darkening'—to use De Vaucouleurs' expression—which spreads from the poles through to low latitudes. Originally they were believed to be seas, but this theory is disposed of at once by the paucity of water-vapour in the atmosphere. We can also reject the suggestion by S. Arrhenius[10] that hygroscopic salts are responsible—that is to say, salts which pick up moisture and darken in the process. There simply is not enough moisture on Mars, bearing in mind that the dark patches cover vast areas.

A somewhat improbable-sounding theory was proposed in 1954 by D. B. McLaughlin,[11] according to which the patches are due to ash ejected at intervals by active volcanoes. Since this idea explains none of the established phenomena, such as the seasonal darkening, and moreover there is no cause to assume large-scale vulcanism on Mars, it need detain us no further.

Much of the evidence available suggests that the patches are due to 'plant-like' life—probably of a lowly kind, no more advanced than terrestrial lichens or mosses, but capable of responding to the arrival of moisture from the shrinking polar caps.

One interesting fact is that the Martian atmosphere seems to be unexpectedly opaque to light of short wavelength, and this has been attributed to the so-called *violet layer*, lying at perhaps 8 miles above the surface of the planet. Sometimes this violet layer clears for a period, and there is no longer so strong a shield against the ultra-violet radiation emitted by the Sun. During one such clearing, in 1941, S. L. Hess carried out some experiments which suggested that the seasonal development of the dark areas was halted. This has been held to show that the plant life was being damaged by the solar ultra-violet bombardment.

Not all astronomers agree with the 'plant' hypothesis. For instance, V. V. Sharonov[12] has advanced a theory according to which the processes of weathering and denudation on Mars, due to the absence of water and oxygen, give rise to large quantities of fine dust; dark regions are considered as areas of formation and deflation of this dust, while the bright areas are regarded as the areas of its accumulation. It would certainly be premature to claim that the matter is definitely settled.

The Bright Areas. The reddish-ochre regions which cover so much of Mars are commonly called 'deserts', but are in no way similar to the deserts of Earth. They are of course cold— colder, indeed, than the dark patches—and are certainly not sandy. It seems that the surface is coated with some reddish mineral, possibly felsite or limonite. A Martian desert must be remarkably bleak and unfriendly.

The Canals. Mars has always been the favourite planet of the story-tellers, who delight in populating it with all manner of life-forms. Formerly it was believed that activity might be observable there. Who has not heard of the Martian 'canals'?

In 1877 G. V. Schiaparelli, observing at Milan with an $8\frac{3}{4}$-in. refractor, recorded numbers of fine, straight lines crossing the reddish-ochre areas. He termed them *canali* or channels, and regarded it as possible that they were artificial waterways, built by intelligent Martians to convey water from the snowy poles through to the arid equatorial zone. He also found that some of the canals showed abrupt doubling, so that two parallel lines would appear where previously only one had been seen. After 1886 the strange features were reported by other observers also, and Percival Lowell, who founded the Flagstaff Observatory in Arizona mainly to study Mars, mapped hundreds between 1895 and his death in 1916. Lowell was convinced that intelligent activity was responsible, and even wrote:[13] 'That Mars is inhabited by beings of some sort or other we may consider as certain as it is uncertain what these beings may be.'

However, later work has led to the almost universal rejection

of this attractive idea. Few modern astronomers see the canals
in the form described by Lowell; more generally they are described (if seen at all) as broad, irregular streaks, not in the least
artificial in appearance. Dollfus[14] regards the 'Lowell-type'
canals as purely physiological, produced by the well-known
tendency of the human eye to join up disconnected features
into straight lines; he also considers that under excellent
conditions of seeing, the canals break down into separate spots
and patches. In any case, it is now known that the polar caps
are too thin to supply enough water for even one really long
canal.

The canal argument still rages. There can be no doubt that
some of the broader streaks, such as the Nilosyrtis, have real
existence, but the presence of finer canals is very much in
doubt. In any case, there is no reason to suppose that they are
artificial, and they are more probably due to the same material
as that which makes up the dark areas.

Biological Considerations. If this picture of conditions on
Mars is approximately correct, we can assert with confidence
that some terrestrial organisms—for instance, bacteria which
do not require free oxygen—could survive there in certain localities. We must now ask whether past conditions on Mars would
have favoured biopœsis, and if there is acceptable evidence for
the existence of living organisms on Mars at the present time.

It seems likely, as Urey[15] has suggested, that the Earth,
Venus and Mars all originally had substantial amounts of water
on their surfaces, so that on Mars, as on the Earth, the gradual
synthesis and chemical evolution of carbon compounds could
have progressed. The analysis of light reflected from the dark
areas of Mars failed to reveal the characteristic absorption
spectrum of chlorophyll. In colour, the dark areas are more
bluish than chlorophyll, and unlike chlorophyll they do not
show striking reflection of infra-red radiations. The work of
G. A. Tikhov[16] and his colleagues at the Institute of Astro-
botany at Alma Ata, in Russia, has helped to clarify the position to some extent. Tikhov argued that since the climate of
Mars is cold and the atmosphere rarefied, it would be more
reasonable to compare the spectrum of the dark areas not with

that of ordinary terrestrial plants, but with the spectra of sub-Arctic and high Alpine plants. Investigation showed that there was a close similarity between the spectra of these plants and the Martian dark areas, and Tikhov has suggested that ability to absorb red and infra-red radiations is consistent with adaptation to cold conditions. Kuiper[17] demonstrated a similarity between the Martian spectrum and the spectrum of terrestrial lichens, organisms which will be discussed later.

New evidence supporting the view that organic molecules exist on Mars has been obtained by W. Sinton, [18, 19] who has found absorption bands in the infra-red spectra of the dark areas at 3·4 and 3·67 microns. The band at 3·4 microns is present in the spectra of all terrestrial plants which have been examined, but at first the band at 3·67 microns was something of a mystery. It has since been found in the spectrum of the alga *Cladophora*, and is probably due to the presence of carbohydrate molecules in the organism. Sinton has suggested that this might be an indication that Martian organisms store larger amounts of reserve carbohydrate than do most terrestrial plants, and so show stronger absorption at 3·67 microns.

Nature of the Hypothetical Martian Organisms. If organisms are present on Mars, what are they like? It is perhaps unfortunate that many authors use the term 'vegetation' when referring to Mars in a way which is liable to suggest that organisms such as terrestrial plants may be found. There may, indeed, be similarities between certain terrestrial and Martian organisms, but it is most probable that the Martian 'vegetation' differs in important respects from terrestrial green plants. The absence of free oxygen in the atmosphere is hardly consistent with the release of oxygen resulting from biological photosynthesis. The oxygen released by terrestrial green plants is derived from water, and water is scarce on Mars.

Since life on Mars, as on the Earth, must depend ultimately on solar energy, we may assume that some Martian organisms are equipped with energy-trapping, photosynthetic biochemical systems. It may be, then, that like our terrestrial photosynthetic bacteria, Martian organisms do not release free oxygen in the course of photosynthesis, but re-combine it to form water. An alternative possibility, suggested by H. Strughold,[20] is that organisms resembling terrestrial lichens may exist on Mars. Lichens represent a sort of joint effort at living, a symbiotic combination of alga and fungus—the former 'wrapped up', as it were, in the latter. The algæ produce oxygen in the course of photosynthesis, but in some species the gas can be trapped in the interstices of the fungus, and re-used. Organisms of this kind conserve their own private atmospheres, and the internal concentration of oxygen may be many times greater than that

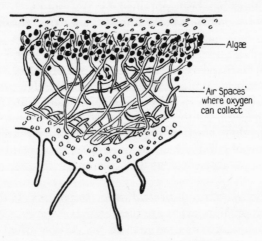

FIG. 23. Section through a Lichen.

in the surrounding air. They are well adapted to survival in dry, rigorous conditions.

The climate of Mars is extreme, but not so very different from the most rigorous places on Earth. The conditions at high altitudes on terrestrial mountains resemble in many respects those at the Martian surface. Many terrestrial micro-organisms are able to withstand extremes of cold—even approaching absolute zero—and yet revive when warmed again; they may remain in a dormant state for long periods. Some organisms may be cooled and revived without damage much more easily than others, and it is, for example, much easier to cool and revive bacteria than more highly organized creatures.[21, 22] It would, however, be possible for some organisms to survive the Martian cold in a dormant state. Martian organisms would have to be resistant to drought, and have efficient means of water conservation, or ability to remain dormant but viable in a dried state. This again is possible, for many terrestrial micro-organisms are highly resistant to drying.

Experiments initiated recently by the authors have demonstrated that some terrestrial bacteria can survive for at least many weeks, and may even multiply to some extent, under simulated Martian conditions. Various micro-organisms were mixed with artificial 'soils', consisting of mixtures of silicates and oxides of iron, and traces of organic 'foods'. These mixtures were placed in containers with an atmosphere of nitrogen and carbon dioxide, at a pressure of about 70 mm. of mercury. Day temperatures were maintained at around 20° C., and at night the temperature was reduced to −76° C. by placing the samples in a dry ice cabinet. So far, only certain bacteria have survived for more than a few days. Algæ and protozoa which were tested soon perished, but there may be some hardier species yet to be discovered. Similar observations have been made by American investigators. In general, we might expect that bacteria would fare best under Martian conditions, and, if our picture of the Martian surface and atmosphere is reasonably correct, there is a real possibility that some terrestrial bacteria could establish themselves there.

Animal Life? It is unlikely that Mars at the present time supports animal life as we know it. It is worth noting here that even if the Martian atmosphere consisted of pure oxygen, an Earthman would still be unable to breathe it. When we breathe, we take air into our lungs, and there it mixes with carbon dioxide and water-vapour which have been produced by the body. The pressure of the internally produced carbon dioxide and water-vapour is more or less constant at about 87 mm. Hg., while at sea-level on the Earth the total atmospheric pressure is about 760 mm. Hg. If the external air pressure is reduced until it equals the internal pressure in the lungs (87 mm. Hg.), then no air can enter the lungs—which are already fully occupied by gas at this pressure. In the Earth's atmosphere, these conditions are found at altitudes of 52,000 feet and above. On Mars, it is likely that the total atmospheric pressure at the surface is about 70 mm. Hg., and it is clear that pure oxygen at this pressure could not be breathed. It seems probable that nitrogen forms the major part of the Martian atmosphere, and of the 70 mm. Hg. total pressure only about 1 mm. is due to oxygen, so that men would need efficient pressurized breathing apparatus for survival.

Given a great enough total atmospheric pressure to permit breathing, most terrestrial warm-blooded animals would fail to survive unless the partial pressure of oxygen in the atmosphere exceeded 60 mm. Hg. Cold-blooded animals manage with less, and may survive periods of oxygen deprivation, with partial pressures of O_2 as low as 5 mm. Hg. Strughold[20] is probably correct in arguing that ability to survive oxygen deprivation does not mean that these animals could have evolved at such low oxygen pressures; some comments by J. R. Nursall[23, 24] are relevant here. It seems most improbable that even cold-blooded animals, built on terrestrial patterns, will be found on Mars.

Conclusions. The belief that Mars is the most likely planet in our Solar System for the existence of extra-terrestrial life is by no means new, and the accumulating evidence suggests that it is probably correct. Further important advances may have to await the landing of instrumented probes. Automatic equipment is being designed which should make possible the sampling and microscopical examination of surface materials of other planets, pictures of the specimens collected and processed being tele-vised back to Earth[25]. We may, therefore, be able to see some extra-terrestrial organisms long before the first astrobiologist sets foot on another world.

It is generally believed that Mars will be found to be, as Spencer Jones[26] has said, 'the planet of ebbing life', but for the present this belief should be held with strong reservations. Strughold has tentatively suggested that the planets *nearer* the Sun may be the biologically 'older' ones. Reactions on these warmer planets would have proceeded faster, and life might have appeared sooner. On this view Venus, if not always too hot, would be a planet where life might have developed and run its course more quickly than on Earth. Mars would still be biologically at an early stage, perhaps not far removed from the dawn of living matter. If this idea were correct, Mars would be of supreme interest as possibly providing evidence for or against some of the theories of biopœsis which have been propounded. It is difficult to assess the plausibility of Strughold's suggestion without more precise details of the history of the Solar System than are yet available.

Survival on Mars. Though Mars could hardly support indigenous life of advanced type, it is much less hostile than the Moon. In time, it will no doubt be reached by expeditions from Earth. A Martian voyage will take months (assuming that the vehicles are powered by chemical rockets), and will be a difficult matter; if it can be accomplished, there is every reason to suppose that our scientific techniques will have advanced far enough to ensure survival on the planet.

The pioneer expedition will presumably have to establish a base, since a period of months must elapse before the return journey can be started. Here, too, the pressurized plastic dome has been suggested, and may be a much more practicable proposition than on the Moon, since the Martian atmosphere is dense enough to act as an efficient meteor-screen.

Many science fiction novels depict explorers walking about Mars, in the hottest part of the day, with no extra protection other than oxygen masks. There is, however, distinct doubt as to whether the atmospheric pressure is enough to prevent the danger of blood-boiling, and it may well be that pressurized suits will always be necessary.

At any rate, the pioneers from Earth will find plenty of problems awaiting their attention. We do not yet know when the first expeditions will set out; but not until they land will we know, without a shadow of doubt, whether Mars is a planet of ebbing life or whether it is a world upon which life, of a kind, still flourishes.

VI

VENUS

Our knowledge of Venus is much less extensive than in the case of Mars. The minimum distance is less, and Venus is a larger body; it is in fact almost the equal of the Earth. Unfortunately, the actual surface can never be seen, since the atmosphere of the planet is all-concealing.

The following table gives the relevant data for Venus:

Data for Venus

Distance from the Sun:	max. 67, 650,000 miles
	mean 67,200,000 ,,
	min. 66,750,000 ,,
Orbital eccentricity:	0·0068
Sidereal period:	224 d. 16 h. 48 m.
Orbital inclination	3° 24'
Diameter:	7700 miles
Volume, Earth = 1:	0·92
Mass, Earth = 1:	0·81
Density, Earth = 1:	0·89
Specific gravity:	4·9
Surface gravity, Earth = 1:	0·85
Escape velocity, miles/sec:	6·3

The orbit is of low eccentricity, but it is impossible to say much about the seasons on Venus, since the axial inclination is not known. G. P. Kuiper, from photographic studies, gives a value of 32 degrees from the perpendicular,[1] but A. Dollfus, working at the Pic du Midi, considers that 'the globe turns upon an axis only slightly inclined to the plane of the orbit'.[2] Other estimates have been made ranging through a complete right angle. It is best to admit that so far, we simply do not know.

Rotation Period. The axial rotation period is equally uncertain. Visual studies are of little use, since the dusky shadings seen on the disk of Venus are too vague and too impermanent to yield

90

reliable results. Moore, who has carried out observational work regularly since 1934, holds the view that the shadings shift and change too rapidly for rotational drifts to become measurable.[3] Kuiper's photographic studies[1] lead him to propose a period of 'a few weeks', but this is disputed by Dollfus,[4] who believes that the period is 224·7 days—in which case Venus, like Mercury, would have a 'captured' rotation, keeping the same hemisphere turned permanently sunward. Radio signals, reported in 1954 by J. D. Kraus at Ohio[5] yielded a period of only 22 hours 17 minutes, but these radio signals have not been detected except by the Ohio team, and it would be unwise to place much reliance on them. Recent Russian work gives a value of 10 days.

The best chance of solving the problem would be to detect Doppler shifts at opposite limbs of the planet. Assuming a moderate axial inclination, one limb would be approaching, and would give a violet shift; the opposite limb would be receding, giving a red shift. So far, however, no such effects have been detected. The most complete investigation has been made by R. S. Richardson,[6] who concludes that the rotation period is longer than in the case of the Earth. In this case it is hardly surprising that the slight Doppler effects are masked by observational errors. In a curious book published in 1957, M. W. Ovenden advanced the theory that Venus rotates inside its atmosphere, so that no Doppler shifts would be expected; he also wrote that 'any large lunar-type craters on Earth would in a few million years be rubbed away by friction with the atmosphere as the Earth rotates underneath it'.[7] Ideas of this sort are, however, based on complete disregard of elementary principles.

One objection to the captured-rotation theory supported by Dollfus is that the temperatures of the bright and dark hemispheres seem to be much the same. Measures by W. M. Sinton and J. Strong[8] give about $-40°$ C.; N. A. Kozyrev, in the U.S.S.R., prefers $-90°$ C.[9] Were the dark side permanently averted from the Sun, we would expect a lower temperature there, though we must always bear in mind that we are dealing only with the temperature of the uppermost part of Venus' atmosphere.

Atmosphere and 'Clouds'. In view of the fact that the escape velocity of Venus does not differ much from that of the Earth, the atmosphere may be expected to be of comparable depth, and this is supported by all available evidence. Spectroscopic studies are limited to the upper layers, and we have no direct information as to conditions lower down, but at least we have something to guide us. The main constituent seems to be carbon dioxide, as was found by Adams and Dunham in 1932,[10] using equipment fitted to the 100-in. Hooker reflector at Mount Wilson. According to Slipher and Adel,[11] the carbon dioxide in the atmosphere of Venus is equal to a layer 2 miles in thickness at standard atmospheric pressure and temperature, as against a mere 30 feet for the Earth. Since carbon dioxide has a marked greenhouse effect, there are immediate reasons for supposing that the surface temperature of the planet is high.

The so-called 'clouds' also present problems. In 1937, R. Wildt proposed that they might be due to formaldehyde (CH_2O), formed under the influence of solar ultra-violet;[12] another theory attributes them to salts such as sodium chloride and magnesium chloride, produced by the drying-up of former oceans. It seems definite, at any rate, that the atmosphere contains particles in violent motion.

In 1954 F. L. Whipple and D. H. Menzel suggested that the 'clouds' might, after all, be due to H_2O.[13] Their work was based on polarization measures made earlier by B. Lyot, at Meudon,[14] which seemed to be incompatible with the idea of dust-clouds, but supported the water-droplet hypothesis. At that time no water-vapour had been detected in the atmosphere of Venus, and the H_2O theory was strongly attacked by E. J. Öpik[15] and others. However, recent observations, made by United States astronomers with instruments carried in a balloon, have led to the discovery of abundant water-vapour, so that Öpik's objections are removed. The H_2O nature of the 'clouds' cannot be said to have been proved, but at least it seems much the most likely explanation.

In 1960, a close examination of spectra of Venus obtained by N. A. Kozyrev and others was carried out by B. Warner, at London University. The results indicate that there is a reasonably strong chance that oxygen exists in the atmosphere of the planet, though once again definite proof is lacking.[16]

Magnetic Field of Venus. Venus seems to possess a strong magnetic field. Near inferior conjunction, when Venus is approximately between the Earth and the Sun, this field would produce effects upon the electrically-charged particles emitted by the Sun, and a long-continued study by J. Houtgast[17] carried out along these lines has led to an estimate of a field five times as powerful as that of the Earth. The celebrated 'Ashen Light', or faint luminosity of the nocturnal hemisphere, may therefore be due to effects in the planet's atmosphere more or less analogous to terrestrial auroræ, a point of view supported by spectrographic researches made by Kozyrev in the Crimea.[18]

In this connection, V. A. Firsoff[19] has suggested that magnetic effects on different gases lead to a tendency for the carbon dioxide to rise above the oxygen, so that the lower layers of the atmosphere of Venus may be unexpectedly oxygen-rich. This theory has been proposed independently by N. Barabashov, Chairman of the Soviet Interplanetary Commission.[20] Whether subsequent research will support it remains to be seen.

Surface Conditions. It is clear that our ideas as to surface conditions on Venus must be based only on indirect evidence. We know that the atmosphere is considerable, and made up largely of carbon dioxide, together with water-vapour and smaller quantities of other gases; we believe the rotation period to be longer than that of the Earth; it is probable that the 'clouds' are of H_2O. Thermal radiation studies made at a wavelength of 3·15 cm. by Mayer, Sloanaker and McCullough at Washington[21] yield a high surface temperature—which is, of course, to be expected. Yet the surface itself is permanently hidden, and current theories may be very wide of the mark.

Earlier in the present century, it was thought that Venus might be a 'Carboniferous-type' world, with abundant plant life of the sort which flourished on Earth between 200 and 250 million years ago, and probably amphibians or even reptiles. S. Arrhenius wrote that 'we must conclude that everything on

Venus is dripping wet. The vegetative processes are greatly accelerated by the high temperature; therefore, the lifetime of organisms is probably short.' The later analysis of the planet's upper atmosphere led to the rejection of Arrhenius' theory, and it was then supposed that Venus must be a dust-desert, without a trace of moisture anywhere. This was the view of E. H. Öpik,[15] H. C. Urey[22] and other authorities, but the detection of abundant water-vapour seems to indicate that it is wrong.

According to Whipple and Menzel,[13] a thick atmosphere consisting largely of carbon dioxide could not exist on an earth-like planet with continents protruding from oceans of water; the carbon dioxide would be fixed in the rocks in the form of carbonates, because of its chemical reaction with silicates in the presence of water. If protruding land masses were absent, however, the fixation of carbon dioxide could not continue after the formation of a thin buffer layer of carbonates. Whipple and Menzel therefore suggest that Venus is completely covered with water.

We cannot come to any final conclusions as to the existence or non-existence of life on Venus until we have a better knowledge of the surface conditions. Though the marine hypothesis appears by far the best, it is certainly not proved, and in any case there may be appreciable land-masses in the form of protruding islands. All we can do is to take the various theories one by one, and see what conclusions may be drawn.

On the dust-bowl theory, life on any terrestrial pattern is clearly out of the question. Arrhenius' picture of luxuriant vegetation and amphibian life seems to be ruled out by the high temperature revealed by radio studies. If Venus is mainly or completely ocean, however, the situation is rather different.

In 1959, Moore suggested[23] that Venus may be a world in a condition similar to the Earth in Cambrian times, about 500 million years ago. At that period, the Earth's atmosphere probably contained more carbon dioxide and less free oxygen than it does now; in fact, it may have been rather similar to the present atmosphere of Venus. The seas contained primitive organisms, ancestors of the later more complex forms, and there is at least a possibility that this stage in biological development has been reached on Venus.

Biological Considerations. The marine theory immediately offers the possibility that many types of living things may exist, and it may be that some of the oxygen of Venus' atmosphere has been derived from the photosynthetic activities of alga-like organisms. In the absence of precise quantitative data on the oxygen content of the atmosphere, speculations on the likely degree of complexity of Cytherean organisms must remain mere guesses. If, however, there is a good deal of oxygen at the surface, many-celled organisms, and even animal life of some sort, may exist.

Unless the surface temperature is prohibitively high, Venus may be at least as interesting biologically as Mars. If the temperature is near the upper limit compatible with the existence of carbon-based organisms, a biologist may reasonably hope to find fascinating examples of adaptation to high temperatures. Strughold's suggestion[24] that the warmer planets could be the 'biologically older' ones, as mentioned in Chapter VI, deserves careful consideration. Life on Venus may not have 'run its course', but there may be advanced forms of life, perhaps all aquatic, suited to the conditions which prevail there. Like terrestrial organisms, Cytherean forms could have produced modifications of the planet's atmosphere.

It is unlikely that organisms well suited for existence on the Earth and on Venus would exactly resemble each other, and it is probable that they would differ in many metabolic details, so that the biological modification of the atmosphere of Venus could differ quantitatively and qualitatively from that which plants and plant-like organisms have produced on Earth.

Within a comparatively few years, Venus will probably be explored by means of instrumented probes and even manned space-craft. These will indeed be exciting days for astronomers and biologists, because only then will the secrets of that modestly-veiled planet be revealed.

VII

OTHER WORLDS OF THE SOLAR SYSTEM

Conditions on Mars and Venus may not be promising for terrestrial-type life, but the other bodies of the Solar System are even less suitable, and may be dismissed relatively briefly.

Mercury. Mercury, the innermost planet, has a diameter of 3100 miles, and is thus not a great deal larger than the Moon. Its mean distance from the Sun is 36,000,000 miles, but the orbit is of some eccentricity, and the distance varies between 29,000,000 miles at perihelion and 43,000,000 miles at aphelion. The sidereal period is 87·9 days which is the same as the period of axial rotation, so that Mercury always presents the same hemisphere to the Sun.

However, the orbital velocity changes between 24 and 36 miles per second, whereas the axial spin is constant. The result is an effect more or less analogous to the Moon's libration, and there is a zone, between the region of permanent day and the region of permanent night, over which the Sun would appear to rise and set. This is known popularly, though rather inaccurately, as the 'twilight zone'. Its precise extent is uncertain, as the angle of inclination of Mercury's axis has still not been properly determined.

We have to admit that, on the whole, we know very little about the surface features of Mercury, E. M. Antoniadi, a Greek astronomer who did most of his work with the 33-in. refractor at Meudon (Paris), drew a map over a quarter of a century ago,[1] and this remains probably the best, though its accuracy is questionable. Dark patches are recorded, and have been named; among the most prominent are the Solitudo

Hermæ Trismegisti and the Solitudo Criophori. Whether they are analogous to the lunar 'seas' remains uncertain, and neither do we know whether the Mercurian surface is mountainous.

The temperatures on the planet must be extreme. Over the hottest part of the 'day' zone, at perihelion, $+ 410°$ C. is the best estimate; the night zone can be little above absolute zero. In the so-called twilight zone, admittedly, temperatures would be modified.

The escape velocity on Mercury is 2·6 miles per second, and hence no extensive atmosphere is to be anticipated. For many years it was indeed thought that Mercury must be devoid of any mantle. However, Audouin Dollfus has announced the detection of a very tenuous atmosphere, with a ground density not exceeding $\frac{3}{1000}$ that of the Earth's. This yields a barometric pressure of about 1 mm., and is to all intents and purposes negligible. It is certainly incapable of conveying appreciable heat from the sunlit to the 'nocturnal' regions.

Satellites and Asteroids. At this point, it is convenient to say something about other worlds in the Solar System which lack effective atmospheres. The Moon, as we have seen, is one such case, and we are entitled to assume that all globes with less than the lunar mass are devoid of atmospheres. The asteroids may be dismissed at once. Ceres, by far the largest of them, has a diameter of only 430 miles and a very low escape velocity, so that it is utterly incapable of retaining even the most tenuous mantle. This applies also to most of the satellites;[2] both the attendants of Mars, eight of Jupiter's family, eight of Saturn's, one of Neptune's, and all five of Uranus'. The largest satellites are listed in the following table:

Name	Primary	Diameter (miles)	Escape Velocity miles/sec.
Titan	Saturn	3500	2·0
Triton	Neptune	3300	2·0
Callisto	Jupiter	3220	0·9
Ganymede	Jupiter	3200	1·8
Io	Jupiter	2310	1·5
Moon	Earth	2160	1·5
Europa	Jupiter	1950	1·3

97

Callisto (which has surprisingly little mass in view of its size), Io and Europa have escape velocities no greater than that of the Moon, and their atmospheres must be negligible. Ganymede, too, seems to be devoid of a mantle. Triton may have a tenuous atmosphere made up of methane, and Titan possesses a methane atmosphere; it was detected spectroscopically by Kuiper in 1944.

Could there be Life on Worlds without Atmospheres? It is highly improbable, if not absolutely impossible, that biopœsis could occur on a body which had never had an atmosphere, or had lost its atmosphere in a short time after formation. The rate at which an atmosphere is lost depends on the escape velocity and temperature. Rise of temperature will increase the velocities of the gas molecules, which will therefore be lost more readily. At its present temperature the Moon could retain some carbon dioxide and other heavier gases, but it would lose lighter gases such as oxygen, hydrogen, helium, nitrogen and water-vapour. The fact that the Moon now seems to be devoid of atmosphere probably indicates loss of even the heavier gases when the Moon was at a higher temperature in the past. Spencer Jones[3] has pointed out that, at a temperature of 1000° C., the Moon would lose an atmosphere of carbon dioxide in a few years. It is possible that the Moon was never as hot as this, so it might have retained some atmosphere for longer. The extremely tenuous lunar atmosphere of the present day may contain traces of sulphur dioxide, and other heavy gases.

An atmosphere has several effects important for chemical and biochemical evolution. It is exposed to the passage of solar radiations, and these promote photochemical reactions. Reactive chemical groups are formed, which react with each other and with surface components. The ability of the changing atmosphere to screen off selectively some radiations, such as ultra-violet regions of the spectrum, may improve conditions for developing organisms and influence the course of later evolution. There is also protection against some primary cosmic radiation. An atmosphere exerts a pressure, and this affects the boiling point of liquids, including water, at the surface and the ability of organisms to make use of atmospheric gases. In an atmosphere, materials can be intermingled and spread over the surface of the globe, and storms and electrical discharges can further influence the direction of chemical change. Life may be regarded as 'woven out of air by light' (Moleschott, quoted by Bernal[4]) and although this is perhaps a rather one-sided epigram, it stresses an important factor.

It seems probable, then, that any organisms which may exist on, or *in*, an airless world, will be descendants of others which were formed at an earlier time when there was an atmosphere. When discussing the Moon (Chapter IV) we stressed the difficulties which would face an organism requiring a water supply. It is perhaps within the bounds of possibility that the major part of an organism might be buried deeply below the surface in areas which still, even intermittently, received some water from a deeper source. Any part of an organism exposed at the surface would have to be impermeable to water, so that the complete organism could remain sufficiently 'pressurized' for liquid water to exist inside it. It is possible, even, to imagine a 'light trap' exposed portion, so that the energy of the light from the star of the system could be used. Stretching the imagination still further, we might picture a process which has, in the course of time, left one self-contained, branching or net-like organism spread over a large area, life being carried on by a repeated cycling of the contents, assisted by light, and all available free water remaining permanently within the impermeable walls of the organism. It is possible that, where radiation exposure had been becoming progressively severe on a world gradually losing its atmosphere, considerable degrees of biological adaptation to high doses of radiations might occur. There is a wide range of variation in sensitivitiy to radiations among terrestrial organisms, and it would be unwise to conclude that greater resistance will not be found in organisms adapted to exposed situations.

In conclusion, it can be said that a completely dry, atmosphere-less world would not give rise to and support indigeneous life. Where an atmosphere had previously existed, and supplies of water were in some way still available, specially adapted descendants of earlier organisms might possibly linger on for a limited time. Life on an airless world would be wholly or partly 'subterranean', and if totally buried would be limited by lack of photosynthesis. Whilst it is possible to imagine types of large organism which might exist, a hardy and biologically resourceful population of micro-organisms might have the best hope of survival, given an intermittent supply of water.

Pluto. The most remote member of the Sun's family of planets is Pluto. It seems to be a small world, with less than half the diameter of the Earth, but it has provided astronomers with a great number of problems.

Certain irregularities in the movements of the two outer giants, Uranus and Neptune, led the American astronomer Percival Lowell—of 'Martian Canal' fame—to suppose that another world must exist at a still greater distance. Lowell calculated where this hypothetical planet must lie, and his results were independently confirmed by W. H. Pickering. Initial searches proved fruitless, but in 1930, fourteen years after Lowell's death, the planet was discovered photographically by Clyde Tombaugh, working at the Flagstaff observatory which Lowell had founded.

Even in large telescopes Pluto appears only as a starlike point; only the Palomar 200-in. reflector has any hope of showing a measurable disk, and diameter measures are consequently uncertain. The best available value, due to G. P. Kuiper, indicates that Pluto is rather smaller than Mars. Unless it is extraordinarily dense, it could not therefore produce appreciable perturbations in the motions of Uranus and Neptune—and yet it was by these very perturbations that Pluto was tracked down. Either the discovery was sheer luck, or else Pluto is larger or more massive than the diameter measures indicate.

Surface details cannot, of course, be made out, and a telescope of fair power is needed to show Pluto at all. Periodical variations in magnitude have led to a derived rotation period of 6 days 9 hours, but this cannot be regarded as really reliable.

It is difficult to believe that Lowell's successful prediction was purely fortuitous, and equally difficult to believe in a very high density. A suggestion due originally to A. C. D. Crommelin, in 1936, may provide an answer. What Kuiper has measured may not be the full diameter of Pluto; specular reflection may play an important part, in which case the planet may be much larger than Mars and possibly even larger than the Earth. Kuiper himself is inclined to the view that Pluto is not a genuine planet at all, but a former satellite of Neptune which somehow moved away in an independent orbit.

It is certainly true that the present orbit is unusual. The eccentricity is relatively high (0·247), and at perihelion the distance from the Sun is only 2766 million miles—less than the minimum distance of Neptune. The mean distance of 3666 million miles is, however, much greater, and the sidereal period amounts to 247·7 years. Owing to the sharper inclination of Pluto's orbit (17°), a direct encounter with Neptune is unlikely to the highest degree, at least in the foreseeable future.

The temperature of the surface must be in the region of − 240° C., a figure which would appear to preclude the existence of any conceivable form of life. The uncertainty as to the diameter and mass means that we have no positive information on the escape velocity, but any atmosphere would have to be composed of gases with a very low liquefaction point. No atmosphere has been found, but its detection would of course be a matter of extreme difficulty.

From Pluto the Sun would appear small, though brilliant enough to cast a light much more powerful than that of our full Moon. Of the other planets, only Neptune, and at times Uranus, would be visible with ease. Conventional maps of the Solar System tend to mask the fact that at its average distance from the Sun, Pluto is considerably further away from Uranus than we are.

Many of the problems set by this remote, cold little world remain to be cleared up, but it is so obviously unsuited for life that in the present context we need discuss it no further.

The Giant Planets. The four giant planets are worlds very different in type from those previously discussed. Jupiter and Saturn have been known from antiquity; Uranus was discovered in 1781 by Herschel, and Neptune in 1846 by Galle and D'Arrest, as a result of calculations made by the French mathematician U. J. J. Le Verrier (independent calculations by John Couch

Adams, of Cambridge, had led to a similar result). The relevant data may be summarized as follows:

Planet	Mean Distance from Sun, Millions of miles	Sidereal Period, yrs	Equatorial Diameter, miles	Mass, Earth = 1
Jupiter	483·3	11·86	88,700	318
Saturn	886·1	29·46	75,100	95
Uranus	1783	84·01	29,300	15
Neptune	2793	164·79	27,700	17

	Density, Water = 1	Rotation Period (Equatorial)	Temperature °C.
Jupiter	1·3	9 h. 50 m.	−130
Saturn	0·7	10 h. 14 m.	−150
Uranus	1·3	10 h. 48 m.	−190
Neptune	2·2	14 h. ±	−220

The low densities, less than that of water in the case of Saturn, are very significant. We have to confess that we are uncertain as to the interior structure of a giant planet; according to R. Wildt the general picture is of a rocky core, surrounded by a layer of ice which is in turn overlaid by a deep atmosphere. An alternative theory due to W. R. Ramsey suggests that a giant planet consists mainly of hydrogen, so compressed near the centre of the globe that it assumes metallic characteristics. At any rate, the outer gases may be analyzed, and are found to be very rich in hydrogen, together with hydrogen compounds such as ammonia and methane, plus some helium.

Jupiter is a splendid object in even a small telescope, since its disk shows considerable detail. The famous 'cloud belts', which may be formed by droplets of liquid ammonia, are prominent, and there are also spots, streaks and festoons. The only semi-permanent disturbance is the Great Red Spot, which has been seen at intervals ever since 1631, and was very prominent for some years following 1878; it is still visible. B. M. Peek[5] considers that it may be a mass of solid helium, and that its variations in conspicuousness are due to slight changes in its depth below the outer surface.

Unusual phenomena are also to be seen now and then. In 1959, for instance, Moore detected a curious yellow-orange colour covering much of the equatorial zone, giving the general impression of a high-altitude obscuration; this was abundantly confirmed, but had disappeared when Jupiter became visible once more in 1960.

Jupiter does not rotate as a solid body. The period is shortest at the equator, and increases by several minutes nearer the poles. Visual observations have led to accurate measures of the periods of the various zones, while specific features, such as the Great Red Spot, have periods of their own.

Owing to Jupiter's great mass, the surface gravity is high—2·64 times that of the Earth. However, this is of theoretical interest only, in the present context, since the visible surface is gaseous. Whether there is an actual 'solid boundary' lower down is a matter for debate. It is certain that the density must increase fairly rapidly with increasing depth.

Saturn. Saturn is essentially similar to Jupiter. Belts exist, and there are occasional spots, the most famous of recent years being the white spots of 1933 and 1960. The temperatures are naturally lower, owing to the greater distance from the Sun, and the surface gravity is less—1·2 times that of the Earth. There is an even greater difference between the equatorial and polar rotation periods. The celebrated rings, so lovely when seen through a telescope, are of negligible mass, and are composed of numerous small particles—perhaps ices—circling the planet in the manner of dwarf moons. It has been suggested that the rings were indeed formed by the disruption of a former satellite which came within Roche's limit for Saturn.

Uranus and Neptune. Uranus and Neptune may be regarded as twins, though Neptune is rather the smaller and more massive of the two. Surface features are very hard to make out, but the existence of Jovian-type belts seems fairly well established. Uranus is peculiar inasmuch as its axial tilt is very high—more than a right angle, so that the 'seasons' there are extraordinary. First much of the northern hemisphere, then much of the southern, will experience a 'night' of 21 years, with a corresponding 'midnight sun' in the opposite hemisphere. The reason for this high inclination is unknown. The surface gravity of Uranus is about the same as that of the Earth, while that of Neptune is appreciably greater.

All the giant planets are extremely cold, their surfaces are gaseous, and it is by no means certain that they have cores which are 'solid' in the generally accepted sense of the word. Advanced life of the kind with which we are familiar is clearly out of the question. However, we will now examine matters a little more closely.

Jupiter. In spite of the fact that Jupiter would be wholly unsuitable for terrestrial organisms, its constitution might offer certain interesting chemical possibilities. Haldane[6] has pointed out that there is a whole system of inorganic and organic chemistry in which liquid ammonia takes the place of water. At some levels in the Jovian sphere, liquid ammonia presumably exists, so that there is a formal possibility of a low-temperature chemical evolution which might have some general similarity to that of the higher temperature water-carbon systems. Haldane even threw out the suggestion that a plant-like stage might have been reached on Jupiter. Lederberg[7] considers that the abundance of light elements in the atmosphere of Jupiter, subject to solar radiation at low temperatures and in a high gravitational field 'offers the most exciting prospects for novel biochemical systems'.

Briggs[8] has recently suggested that the reddish-brown colours sometimes seen on Jupiter could be due to the formation of coloured organic compounds from atmospheric constituents by the action of electric discharges. The coloured compounds would tend to react with atmospheric hydrogen to give colourless products. This would account for the periodic fading of the colours, if electric discharges were not frequent enough to keep up the supply of coloured materials.

Saturn, Uranus and Neptune. These planets seem even less likely than Jupiter to be able to support any form of indigenous life. Saturn is so cold that even ammonia probably does not exist to any great extent in the liquid form, and the conditions

104

on Uranus and Neptune are even more severe. We can probably safely conclude that these planets are lifeless worlds.

The structure of the giant planets will probably remain obscure until exploration of Jupiter by means of instrumented probes becomes possible. The automatic collection of samples of the Jovian atmosphere and the return of these to the Earth for analysis should help to settle some of the uncertainties, but this is probably not a feat for the near future. For the present, we have to make the best use we can of the small amount of information available, but this is sufficient to suggest that while the biologist may be unlucky, there will be plenty to interest the chemist when the first samples arrive.

Meteorites. About 90 per cent of the meteorites which reach the Earth are stony (aerolites) and the rest iron (siderites). Most of the iron and stony meteorites would appear to be unlikely sources of traces of living things, but the same may not be true of the carbonaceous chondrites, of which about twenty have been recovered during the last 200 years. Recent investigations by American scientists (see Claus and Nagy, *Nature*, Nov. 18,1961) have provided suggestive evidence that some of these, including the famous Orgueil Meteorite, might contain organic materials and even microfossils. The supposed microfossils resemble certain terrestrial microscopic algæ, and one type unlike any known terrestrial species was also found.

At present, not enough information is available to permit far-reaching conclusions. It is possible that the meteorites (and asteroids) were produced by the break-up of a former planet. If, therefore, the above findings are substantiated, they may provide the first positive evidence for the existence of living things on a planet other than the Earth, and the microfossils would be of great interest and importance.

VIII

PLANETS OF OTHER STARS

So far this book has dealt mainly with possible life on planets in our Solar System. However, this is only part of the problem. The Sun is a normal star, and other stars may have planetary systems of their own.

Origin of the Planets. As was mentioned in Chapter I, the number of stars known to us is immense. Our Galaxy alone includes about 100,000 million. The Sun is of spectral type G, and G-stars are common. We cannot of course maintain that stars which are centres of planetary systems must necessarily be of type G; but first let us examine some of the theories which have been advanced to account for the genesis of the planets.

In 1755, Immanuel Kant advanced a 'gas-cloud' theory. The famous Nebular Hypothesis put forward by P. Laplace in 1796 differs in many ways from Kant's, but for our present purpose the two may be considered together.

According to these ideas, the Solar System began as a large, slowly rotating, contracting nebula. As the nebula shrank under gravitational influences, it shed a series of concentric rings; the material in each ring condensed into a planet, so that the outer planets (Pluto and Neptune) were the first formed, and the innermost (Mercury) the last. The Sun itself is said to represent the remains of the old nebula.

Unfortunately this theory does not stand up to mathematical analysis. As was shown by H. N. Russell in 1895, the angular momentum distribution is wrong. The planets carry 98 per cent of the total angular momentum of the Solar System, while on the nebular hypothesis the Sun would retain by far the larger part. There are other objections as well, and the whole theory has now been rejected.

Another idea, put forward by Chamberlin and Moulton at

106

the beginning of the present century, attributed the formation of the planets to the action of a passing star, which drew material off the Sun; this material accumulated into planets. A variant of the same principle, due to Jeans, assumed that the drawn-off material formed a tongue or cigar-shaped filament. This sounds plausible enough at first sight, particularly since the largest planets (Jupiter and Saturn) lie in the middle part of the system, where the thickest part of the 'cigar' would have been. A grazing collision between the Sun and the passing star has also been suggested, originally by A. W. Bickerton and later by H. Jeffreys.

The passing-star hypothesis remained popular for some time, but objections have been raised which appear to be insuperable. The main trouble is that under the conditions prevailing after such an encounter, it would be impossible for the torn-off material to condense into large planets; it would simply be dissipated.

F. Hoyle formerly maintained that the Sun used to be a binary star, and that the companion underwent a supernova explosion; the recoil led to the final parting of the two bodies, and the last stages of the outburst ejected material which was retained by the Sun and led to the formation of planets. This theory is difficult to disprove, but has never met with much support, and has now been abandoned by its originator.

Two theories proposed since the war, by C. F. von Weizsäcker and by O. Schmidt in Russia, seem to be more promising. According to von Weizsäcker, the Sun was formerly surrounded by a disk-shaped nebula agitated by turbulent vortices. Accretion took place in the zones between large eddies, and gradually the planets were built up. Schmidt's hypothesis is of the same type, though its suggested mechanism is different. On the other hand, G. P. Kuiper has suggested that the Solar System originally consisted of two masses—an embryo binary system—but whereas one mass condensed into the Sun, the other spread out and formed the planets. H. Alfvén, of Sweden, prefers a magneto-hydrodynamic theory, according to which the planets were formed, by magnetic influences, out of a gas-cloud surrounding the Sun.

Frequency of Planetary Systems. This is not the place to

describe the various hypotheses in detail, but one question is important in our present discussion: are planetary systems likely to be common, or are they celestial freaks?

Collisions or close encounters between two stars must be exceptional, even in the most crowded parts of a galaxy. On the average, according to Jeans, a star would meet with such an experience only once in perhaps 500 thousand million million years. This figure has been questioned; but it is clear that if the passing star theory were correct, the Sun's family of planets might be the only one in the Galaxy. Planetary systems would also be rare, though to a less extreme degree, on Hoyle's sypernova hypothesis.

Yet if we follow von Weizsäcker, Schmidt or Alfvén, as most modern astronomers do, the whole situation is altered. What can happen to the Sun can happen to other stars also, particularly since gaseous nebulæ and interstellar clouds in general are very abundant. There is no reason why many, if not the majority, of solar-type stars should not be centres of planetary systems. Neither is there any valid reason to suppose that stars of earlier or later spectral type should necessarily be unattended.

It seems, then, that planetary systems are by no means freakish, and are probably very widespread. This means that inhabited worlds also are likely to be common.

Binary Stars as Planetary Centres. Certain classes of stars, however, are presumably less suited to be associated with life-bearing planets. Some binaries are cases in point. It is now known that binary systems are almost as frequent as single stars; the separations range from virtual contact up to half a light-year or more. With the famous eclipsing star Beta Lyræ, for instance, the components are so close that they almost touch, and each is drawn out into an ellipsoidal shape, while streams of gas pass from one member to the other. In other cases, the separations are so wide that to all intents and purposes we may treat the two components as single stars which merely happen to be unusually close to each other on the stellar scale. The periods of binaries range from a few hours up to over 10,000,000 years. It used to be thought that a binary system was produced by the fission of a single star, but this theory has now become unpopular, and it is regarded as more likely that the components of a binary were born separately in the same region of space.

A very close binary might conceivably have a planetary system, though the orbits of the planets would be complex, and great extremes of surface temperature would be experienced. With separations of, say, more than an astronomical unit, conditions for the birth and survival of planets would be unfavourable. With very wide binaries, however, these objections are removed, since the planets of one component would not be greatly affected by the other.

Planets of binary or multiple-star systems would have complicated paths, depending on the relative masses and separation of the components. In some of the possible orbits, the distances of planets from their 'suns' would vary greatly, so that climatic conditions over such a planet would be most uncomfortable. Long periods of cold, with temperatures low enough to liquefy or solidify water and many gases, would preclude the existence of active forms of life. Yet it is by no means impossible that living things might exist under such conditions. The processes of biopœsis and evolution could proceed during the periods of sufficient warmth, and organisms would remain dormant throughout the long cold seasons. In some cases, however, the closest approach of planet and 'sun' might be near enough to raise the temperature sufficiently to break down complicated carbon compounds, so that life would never be able to emerge.

Variable Stars. Variable stars are of various kinds. Some, such as the Cepheids and RR Lyræ stars, are perfectly regular, so that their changes in brilliancy may be predicted with complete confidence; others, such as Mira Ceti, are of longer period, and are less regular; yet others are irregular, so that we never know how they are going to behave. Here again, it cannot be said that planetary systems are out of the question—but a planet moving round a variable star would experience great ranges of temperature, and life could hardly be expected to flourish under such conditions. These arguments do not, of course, apply to stars which are technically 'variable' but whose changes in output are very slight.

Detection of Planetary Systems. All the evidence we have, indirect though it may be, suggests that systems of planets are quite common in the universe. Unfortunately, no telescope yet built is capable of showing them. The Palomar reflector would be inadequate to reveal a planet the size of Jupiter attending the nearest star. When we are able to set up telescopes beyond the Earth's atmosphere, either in space or on the Moon, we may learn more from direct studies; meanwhile, we have to use other lines of research.

A massive planet moving round a relatively minor star might be expected to make its presence felt by its gravitational effects upon the parent sun. In 1944 K. A. Strand, of Sweden, announced that he had in fact found such perturbations in the motion of one of our nearest stellar neighbours, 61 Cygni B.

61 Cygni is just visible to the naked eye, and achieved fame in 1838 when it became the first star to have its distance measured by trigonometric parallax. It is about 11 light-years away, and is a binary. Both components are feeble; the brighter (A) has only $\frac{1}{19}$ of the Sun's luminosity, while the revolution period is about 700 years. 61 Cygni comes, then, under the heading of a wide system.

Strand's work showed that the fainter component (B) was 'wobbling' very slightly, and he deduced that it was being affected by a body whose mass was about 15 times that of Jupiter. This is too small a mass for a star, and the body may well be a planet, though direct proof is lacking. We have no idea whether it retains any intrinsic luminosity; at any rate, it is too faint to be seen.

Various other stars have shown similar effects, notably 70 Ophiuchi, where the mass of the secondary body is estimated to be only 12 times that of Jupiter. We need not be surprised that the reported cases concern bodies which are very massive by planetary standards. A body with a mass of, say, the Earth could produce no observable effects on its parent star.

In our discussion of the origin of life on Earth, the importance of temperature, with regard to many of the processes concerned, was stressed. Organic compounds may form from many different starting mixtures of simpler molecules; but for syntheses to occur, a fairly limited temperature range is necessary. In conditions of extreme cold, the reactions would proceed very slowly, whereas a temperature as high as 200° C. would prevent many of the stages of biochemical evolution. A planet the size of the Earth orbiting a much hotter star than the Sun, at about the same distance, would be an unlikely site for biopœsis, because of excessive heat. On the other hand, if the star were too cool, the amount of radiation reaching the planet might be too little to permit more than a very slow chemical evolution—and if sufficiently low, might be inadequate for biopœsis.

Planetary Mass and Origin of Life. Planetary mass is important for the processes leading to biopœsis and the later evolution of organisms. The importance of the atmosphere for biochemical evolution is clear, and the constitution of a planet's atmosphere depends on the velocity of escape; as we have seen, massive planets—such as Jupiter and Saturn in our own Solar System—are able to retain hydrogen in their atmospheres, whereas bodies the mass of the Earth or Mars are not.

If a planet of great mass and suitable composition received quantities of radiant energy from a star (and there may be many examples of this in other planetary systems), biogenesis might occur. The course of chemical and biological evolution would be influenced by the retention of hydrogen, but this in itself would not preclude the existence of organisms. To most terrestrial organisms, hydrogen is merely an inert gas, but some micro-organisms are able to utilize molecular hydrogen, while others generate it in the course of their metabolism. There is little doubt, therefore, that organisms similar in general principle to terrestrial forms might develop. The high gravity would influence the forms of any large, complex organisms, so that creatures which could move would have to be rather squat and powerful. Speculations about form must necessarily be wild, but it may be that the vast range of possible carbon compounds includes some which could contribute to much more efficient muscular or contractile organs than we find on Earth.

111

Conversely, on planets with weaker gravitational fields than the Earth's, any advanced forms of life which developed might be relatively taller and less massive.

Attempts at Communication. It may seem surprising, at our present stage of development, that serious attempts were initiated recently, by F. Drake at Green Bank, Virginia, to establish contact with intelligent beings on planets of other stars. These experiments would probably have been unfruitful, but although they have now been discontinued, they were at least interesting.

Apart from the Sun, all the stars are—as we have seen— extremely remote. Moreover, most of our nearest stellar neighbours are unlikely to possess planetary systems comparable with our own. If we examine the stars within 11 light-years of the Sun, we find that all except eight are very feeble red dwarfs of spectrum M. We can also exclude Sirius B, which is a white dwarf, and Procyon B, which is probably a white dwarf. The remainder are as follows:

Star	Distance in light-years	Spectrum	Luminosity, Sun = 1
Alpha Centauri A	4·3	G0	1·1
Alpha Centauri B	4·3	K5	0·2
Sirius	8·6	A0	26
Tau Ceti	10·2	K0	0·35
Procyon	10·4	F5	5·5
Epsilon Eridani	10·5	K0	0·31

Excluding M-type red dwarfs, the next nearest star is Epsilon Indi, which lies at 11·6 light-years and is of spectrum K5, with a luminosity of 0·17 of that of the Sun. However, if we are to contact beings in other systems, we must obviously begin as near home as we can, so let us look carefully at the stars in our list to evaluate the chance of any of them being associated with an inhabited planet.

The choice is easy enough. Alpha Centauri is an unsuitable kind of binary system; Sirius seems to be much too luminous, and this may also apply to Procyon, though less definitely. We are left, then, with Tau Ceti and Epsilon Eridani.

Both these stars are of later spectral type than the Sun, and are less luminous, but on the stellar scale the discrepancies are

112

not really major. There is certainly nothing to prevent either or both from having a planetary system. Whether any of these hypothetical planets are suitable for life, primitive or advanced, is of course quite another matter.

There is only one possible way of communicating with beings at such a distance: by radio methods. The obvious wavelength to select is 21·1 cm., since this is a wavelength of fundamental importance in the Galaxy.

We know that interstellar gas is abundant, and that hydrogen is the main constituent. This hydrogen tends to collect into huge clouds some 30 light-years in diameter, and is at a very low temperature, around −150° C. Naturally it is very rarefied, and optical telescopes will not show it at all. Nevertheless, it emits radio energy at 21·1 cm., as was shown theoretically by Van de Hulst in 1944 and confirmed experimentally by Ewen and Purcell after the end of the war. Radio measures of the interstellar hydrogen have given information as to the distribution of the clouds which lie in the spiral arms of the Galaxy; it is in this way that the spiral structure of the Galaxy has been proved beyond doubt.

This is a fundamental wavelength, and is not affected by the nature of our own equipment or measures. If other races exist, and are as advanced scientifically as ourselves, they will be familiar with the emission from interstellar hydrogen, and with their own radio telescopes they will be studying it.

Two suggestions may be put forward. It might be thought worth while to make regular observations at 21·1 cm. in the hope of detecting signals which form any sort of regular pattern, and must therefore be non-natural. Alternatively, transmissions from Earth might be made on the same wavelength; if picked up in a distant system, replies could be sent in the same way. Intelligible messages would be out of the question, but the very detection of signals would revolutionize all our theories as to the scattering of life in the Galaxy.

These, then, were some of the methods which were adopted at Green Bank with the 85-ft. radio telescope there. The programme was started in 1960, and concentrated chiefly on Tau Ceti and Epsilon Eridani.

One difficulty is that although radio waves travel at the same speed as light, it would take over 10 years for a signal to reach either Tau Ceti or Epsilon Eridani and another 10 years for a reply to be received. Even if success were immediate, it would be 1980 before any response could be received to a transmission sent out in 1960.

It is fair to say that the whole scheme was 'the longest of long shots'. We have no idea whether either of these stars has a system of planets, or whether any such planet is inhabited. Even if we could be sure about these points, the chances of establishing contact would still be remarkably slight. Yet the experiment had at least a scientific basis, and it is a measure of our changed attitude that the programme was considered worth initiating at all.

IX

ALIEN LIFE?

In this book, we have so far confined ourselves to life of the sort familiar to us. There are, however, rather broader concepts which must be dealt with in some detail.

Let us suppose that somewhere in our Galaxy there exists a planet which has an atmosphere less dense than our own, but denser than that of Mars; where the gravity is about half that of the Earth, and where the mean temperature is considerably lower, either because the central star is feebler than our Sun or else because the distance of the planet from its star is greater than our 93,000,000 miles. Conditions of this kind might lead to the development of life; there seems good reason to suppose that they would. Intelligent beings might also appear. They would differ somewhat from terrestrial life-forms, for they would be adapted to live with a thinner atmosphere and under conditions of lower gravity. The suggestion that somewhere in the universe there may be a race of intelligent beings with three heads each and a dozen legs is not necessarily absurd. It would be sheer conceit on our part to maintain that *Homo sapiens* must be the ideal model for life on other worlds.

Yet our hypothetical three- or four-headed, multilegged creatures would be made up of the same elements as we are. Like ourselves, they would require an adequate supply of oxygen and water, and a restricted range of environmental temperature. Suitable conditions do not seem to obtain on Mars, or for that matter anywhere in our Solar System apart from on the Earth.

Fantastic Ideas. It is when we depart from established scientific principles that we enter the realm of fantasy, and this brings us to the fictional creatures known popularly and graphically as 'bug-eyed monsters'. The most famous are those in H. G. Wells' classic novel *The War of the Worlds*, which describes an invasion

115

of the Earth by hostile beings from Mars. Wells' own account reads as follows:

'They were, I now saw, the most unearthly creatures it is possible to conceive. They were huge round bodies—or, rather, heads—about four feet in diameter, each body having in front of it a face. This face had no nostrils—indeed, the Martians do not seem to have had any sense of smell—but it had a pair of very large dark-coloured eyes, and just beneath this a kind of fleshy beak. . . . In a group round the mouth were sixteen slender, almost whip-like tentacles, arranged in two bunches of eight each. . . .'

Wells, of course, never meant his book to be anything more than pure fiction. He has had many followers, but few authors write with his skill, and most of the more recent 'bug-eyed monsters' are disgusting without being entertaining.

Fiction apart, there are many people who have suggested that Wellesian bug-eyed monsters may really exist elsewhere in the universe—perhaps even on Mars. Of course, we cannot be dogmatic enough to say that a bug-eyed monster is an impossibility; our knowledge of the universe is still much too limited. However, it is only wise to collect all the information which we have and put the most rational interpretation on it. There is no scientifically acceptable evidence that bug-eyed monsters exist; consequently, we can relegate them to the place where they belong—between the covers of a science-fiction novel.

Flying Saucers. Perusal of some of the books and articles published during the last two decades shows us that we cannot afford to laugh at the credulous folk who were deceived by Locke's lunar hoax of more than a century ago.

Flying saucers, more respectably known as UFO's, or Unidentified Flying Objects, first came into the news in 1947, when an American business man flying in a private aircraft reported a chain of strange flying objects which he could not identify. Further reports followed, and soon 'Saucers' were all the rage. It was inevitable that the stories should become more and more wild, and before long came the first accounts of meetings with extra-terrestrial beings who had come to Earth to distribute sweetness and light in all possible directions. A Mr.

Truman Bethurum, for instance, announced that he had spent some time on a Saucer from the planet Clarion, captained by a beautiful woman named Mrs. Aura Rhanes. Clarion is not a planet known to astronomers, and though Mr. Bethurum's work was carefully sub-titled 'Non-fiction. A true story of personal experience', it was hardly convincing.

Mr. Bethurum was soon joined by others. Mr. George Adamski, who lives near Palomar mountain in California, wrote his own account of a meeting with men and women from Venus, who landed conveniently nearby, but who did not have the courtesy to pay a call on the Palomar Observatory. Later, Mr. Adamski described his various trips in Saucers, and related his conversations with people from Venus, Mars and even Saturn(!). Most unfortunately, photographs of Saucers are always blurred, and Mr. Adamski's pictures show a vehicle which bears an uncanny resemblance to an electric lamp shade. In 1954 came a British book, 'Flying Saucers from Mars', in which a Mr. Cedric Allingham described his meeting with a Martian who landed on the coast of Scotland. If Mr. Allingham's photograph of his visitor is to be relied upon, it at least shows that the Martians, like ourselves, keep their trousers up by means of braces.

The crop of Saucer books is indeed fantastic. They are of various kinds; accounts of conversations with Superior Beings from other planets, descriptions of the mechanics of space-vehicles, and even pseudo-religious mumbo-jumbo. In some cases it is suggested that the military authorities know all about these visitations, and are deliberately suppressing information; *The Flying Saucer Conspiracy*, by an American writer named Donald Keyhoe, is typical of these. It is also maintained that Venusians, Martians, Saturnians and their kind are living amongst us, masquerading as Earthmen.

Some of the books and stories are obvious hoaxes. Many of the writers, however, seem to be quite sincere—as sincere as the earnest and whole-hearted Flat Earth enthusiasts and astrologers. The whole cult is fascinating psychologically, and is still widespread, even though it is now clearly on the wane.

To discuss flying saucers and bug-eyed monsters further would be pointless. Yet, on a saner level, have we any cause to believe that all life, wherever in the universe it may be found, is built upon the pattern so familiar to ourselves?

Chemical Considerations and Theories of Alien Life

We know that carbon is a suitable element for the formation of 'backbones' of large molecules found in living matter, and the only organisms of which we have experience are carbon-based. It has sometimes been suggested that other related elements might be able to behave in a similar way, so that organisms could be formed on a different basis. The ability of carbon atoms to form chains, often of great length, and rings, is essential to their functioning as the structural basis of 'biological' molecules. Hydrogen, too, has certain unique properties, arising from the smallness of the hydrogen atoms and their related ability to form hydrogen bonds. The latter are essential for the maintenance of the shapes of protein and nucleic-acid molecules. It seems unlikely that any other element could satisfactorily replace hydrogen in carbon-based organisms, and, furthermore, the special properties of water which are of profound biological significance are dependent on the structure of the hydrogen atom. Even the isotope deuterium, differing only by the addition of a neutron to the nucleus, is not biochemically equivalent to hydrogen, and may be inhibitory to growth of organisms, probably because 'deuterium bonds' differ in strength from ordinary hydrogen bonds.

Silicon-Based Life? Silicon has often been suggested as a substitute for carbon, and there are certain similarities between the two elements which may at first appear promising. Both form chains, although in this respect carbon far excels silicon in length and stability of the chains formed. The outermost occupied electron shell in each contains four electrons, and this provides the basis for some rather similar chemical reactions. For instance, carbon and hydrogen can form methane, CH_3, and carbon and silicon form silane, SiH_4. There are large numbers of carbon compounds which have counterparts in silicon chemistry, for example C_2H_6, Si_2H_6; CH_3OH, SiH_3OH, and there are some mixed compounds such as CH_3SiH_2OH; this particular com-

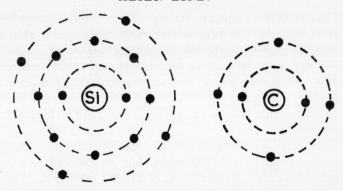

FIG. 24. Electronic structure of silicon (Si) and carbon (C) atoms.

pound resembles ethyl alcohol, CH_3CH_2OH, except that one carbon atom has been replaced by a silicon atom.

In spite of these similarities, there are important differences between carbon and silicon which may rule out the existence of silicon-based organisms. The silicon atom has a greater radius than the carbon atom, the four outermost electrons being in the M shell, whereas in the smaller carbon atom they are in the L shell. Consequently, the outlying electrons of silicon are less strongly attracted by the nucleus than are those of carbon. In carbon dioxide, CO_2, the molecules do not link together, but when silicon is combined with oxygen, the weaker attraction of the nucleus for the outermost electrons permits an oxygen atom to be shared between two silicon atoms, leading to the formation of a crystalline solid in which the atoms are firmly bound together. Silicon dioxide is therefore physically quite different from carbon dioxide, for it is a solid with a very high melting point and low solubility. It is found naturally in the form of sand, quartz and fused silica. In carbon-based organisms, carbon dioxide performs essential functions, but clearly silicon dioxide, which is gaseous only above 2500° C., could not play a similar rôle in water-dependent organisms.

The ability of the M electron shell, of principal quantum number 3 (see p. 11) to accommodate $2n^2 = 2 \times 9 = 18$ electrons introduces further differences between silicon and carbon compounds, for in carbon the outermost (L) shell, of principal quantum number 2, cannot accommodate more than

8 electrons. When carbon is sharing electrons with each of four other atoms, the resulting 'octet' of electrons is not able to 'expand' to receive further electrons. The related silicon compounds are more open to attack, and chains of silicon atoms may be attacked by water, with the result that the Si—Si—Si sequence is changed to Si—O—Si. Carbon forms strong bonds with itself, so that there is an enormous variety of stable organic compounds.

Under great pressures, water and silicon compounds might perhaps coexist in a liquid state, but exactly what would happen under these conditions is at present uncertain. Wilder speculations about silicon organisms living at furnace temperatures and thinking at lightning speed have been tempered by a more realistic appraisal of the properties of silicon and carbon. The chemistry of carbon compounds has, however, been studied in much greater detail than silicon chemistry, and surprises may yet be in store. Silicon-based systems might exhibit some properties similar to those of carbon-based organisms, but the analogy is unlikely to be complete. Mixed forms, containing both carbon and silicon, may offer more scope.

Low Temperature Life? The possibility that organisms might be formed from materials which exist at low temperatures has been mentioned in Chapter VII. It is just possible that carbon-based organisms in which water has been replaced by liquid ammonia might exist at low temperatures. There would obviously have to be many other differences between these and terrestrial organisms, but there is perhaps rather more chance of finding analogous systems at low temperatures than at furnace temperatures.

Sulphur and Oxygen. In the same way that the silicon atom resembles the carbon atom, there is a resemblance between the oxygen and sulphur atoms. In the oxygen atom we find that the K shell contains 2 electrons and the L shell 6. In the sulphur atom the sequence is K,2; L,8; M,6. Again, in spite of the similarity, there are important differences, partly arising from the ability of the M shell in sulphur (as in silicon) to accommodate more than 8 electrons. It seems unlikely that sulphur could play a rôle closely analogous to that of oxygen, as has sometimes been suggested. Sulphur is an important element in carbon-based organisms, and numerous reactions occur in living organisms in which it is involved. It is possible that under other conditions it might be an important factor in some novel kind of high-efficiency metabolic system.

Conclusion. Dogmatism is always to be deplored, and we are almost certainly nearer the beginning than the end of the quest for a full understanding of living things. It is clear that the components of our carbon-based organisms are inter-related in many important ways, and it is difficult to change one part without producing effects which necessitate other changes. Up to the present, suggestions about chemically alien types of organism have not been testable. There seems to be a peculiar 'suitability' in the particular chemical brew which constitutes living things on our own planet, but the very fact of familarity with carbon-based life might increase our difficulty in appreciating the possibility of other forms. The task of formulating alternative systems on paper is one of great complexity, if the result is to be expressed in more than the most general terms. With continuing development in chemical methods and understanding, various theoretical suggestions may, in a century or two, become amenable to laboratory testing, but perhaps before then we may have quite a lot of first-hand information about the other planets of the Solar System, and this may help in a better understanding of the scope and limits of life.

If alien life is possible, and the question is an open one, we may wonder whether or not consciousness will be an attribute of any of these other 'organisms'. Are there, perhaps, different modes of consciousness, associated with different constitutions, and how, if at all, would communication between one type and another be possible? Here we again meet the world of science fiction, and at the moment we can do no more than acknowledge the fascination of these as yet unanswerable questions.

X

SUMMARY OF PRESENT POSITION

We can now look back over the assembled evidence and attempt to draw some conclusions about life in the universe. Any opinions expressed will naturally be tentative, but the recent increase in astronomical knowledge permits some reasoned speculation. We may assert that much detail remains to be filled in, although it seems probable that the general direction of thought on the problem of biopœsis is more or less correctly established.

From one point of view, we can regard 'life' and 'living' as labels we use for the behaviour of matter organized in particular ways. In carbon-based living matter, certain chemical themes regularly recur. In organisms of widely different appearances, there are close similarities in materials and structure at the molecular level, and in the ways in which energy is derived from the environment. We find organisms adapted to various habitats. Some can live at great depths in the sea, others survive on high mountains. Some perish without a supply of free oxygen, whereas others may fail to survive in its presence. There are creatures which can live in desert regions, extraordinarily adept at making the most of small amounts of water available. Certain bacteria may grow even at temperatures near zero Centigrade, and some warm-blooded animals can survive the bitter cold of Arctic and Antarctic conditions. There are bacteria and algæ which prefer high temperatures, even 70° C.; others can grow under conditions of high acidity. Some can withstand loss of a high percentage of their water, becoming inactive until water is again available, and can be revived after exposure to temperatures not much above absolute zero (−273° C.). All these different characteristics seem to be the result of variations on certain basic chemical patterns.

Terrestrial living matter contains various large carbon-based

122

molecules, and we have seen that carbon has certain properties which make it particularly suitable for a rôle of this kind. We may suspect that other elements, even silicon, which is in some ways similar, are unlikely to be able to give rise to molecules of comparable size and similar structure to those of proteins and nucleic acids. This seems to reduce the probability of closely analogous, wholly silicon-based systems.

The evidence we have reviewed suggests that there may be several different sets of conditions under which complex carbon compounds could develop from simpler molecules. Life may be a necessary consequence of certain sets of conditions, and the conditions on the primitive earth were perhaps one suitable set rather than the only possible conditions for biopœsis. Experimental work suggests that the type of atmosphere can be varied, within limits, without preventing, for example, amino-acid production. Moreover, there is good reason to believe that even if life is exclusively carbon-based, organisms appropriate to a rather wide range of planetary conditions might develop. With atmospheric pressures similar to that on the Earth, the upper limit of the tolerable temperature range will be below 100° C., but higher atmospheric pressures would raise the boiling point of water, so that on some planets carbon-based organisms might perhaps be found at temperatures in excess of 100° C. If liquid ammonia can satisfactorily replace water, active low-temperature systems are possible.

It seems most probable that in the observable universe there must be many millions of planets supporting some form of carbon-based life. It is possible that a terrestrial biochemist would be quite at home when investigating many of these organisms, and would find familiar molecules and metabolic sequences in them. There is, of course, plenty of room for surprises, and all sorts of strange compounds and ways of obtaining energy might be encountered.

Patterns of Extra-terrestrial Life. We have remarked that there is an orderliness in chemical reactions. Under a given set of conditions, the probability of some reactions occurring will be greater than that of others. It is by no means impossible that, on planets closely similar to the Earth, chemical and biological evolution might have followed a strikingly similar course, even occasionally to the production of men. The vista opened up is at the same time exciting and tantalizing. There is almost no chance that any of us will know whether the Earth is alone in supporting human life. The only two other planets in our own Solar System which may support some life of terrestrial type do not appear as likely abodes for indigenous men. Interstellar travel to planets of other systems, even by instrumented probes, is not likely to be developed in our lifetimes. Many of us may, however, live to know with certainty whether Mars and Venus support living organisms.

On the other hand, the early formation of some types of organic molecules different from any which formed on the primitive earth might set the course of evolution along rather different lines. We have seen that the constitution of early molecules and organisms to some extent determines the later forms, and an element of 'conservatism' is introduced with the emergence of the first highly successful molecules and systems. Carbon-based organisms on different planets may be similar in principle, but the forms of organisms produced may vary greatly in detail.

Man and Life on Other Worlds. Man is now rapidly acquiring the technical ability to disseminate terrestrial forms of life to other planets, and it is at least possible that intelligent beings in other parts of the universe have, from time to time, attempted space-travel and succeeded. Natural panspermia, leading to the dissemination of organisms over vast interstellar and even inter-galactic distances, is not ruled out, but we have argued that it is beset with numerous hazards. The directed, intelligent spread of life in limited regions of a galaxy, and particularly within individual planetary systems, is a real possibility.

Many micro-organisms can, under suitable conditions, multiply rapidly, and with the help of winds could spread over a planet the size of the Earth in a few weeks. This is the reason for attempts to sterilize probes and space-craft intended for landings on other worlds. If Mars, for example, should be colonized by terrestrial bacteria before a detailed examination of the indigenous organisms had become possible, much valuable scientific information would be lost. The efficient sterilization of space-ships poses difficult technical problems, but both the Russians and Americans are acutely aware of its desirability, and have indicated that adequate precautions will be taken.

The passage of organisms from one planet to another will raise possibilities of biological incompatibility. There is perhaps only a small likelihood that microbes of another planet would produce diseases in terrestrial organisms, but this is by no means impossible. Lederberg,[1] in a discussion of 'exobiology' (a term increasingly used for life beyond the Earth), suggests that harmful organisms from other planets are more likely to be weeds than parasites. Lederberg warns that even a remote possibility of importing dangerous disease-producing organisms from other planets must 'dictate a stringent embargo on the premature return of planetary samples, or of craft that might inadvertently carry them'. On the other hand, there is a danger that the introduction of terrestrial organisms might gravely upset the biological economy of another planet. There are powerful arguments in favour of restraint during early experiments. 'The human species', Lederberg writes, 'has a vital stake in the orderly, careful, and well-reasoned extension of the cosmic frontier; how we react to the adventuresome and perplexing challenge of space-flight will be a crucial measure of the maturity of our national consciences and our concern for posterity.'

Future of Life on Earth. It is clear that life on our Earth cannot continue indefinitely. We depend upon the Sun, and any appreciable changes in the output of solar energy would make the Earth uninhabitable. Even an alteration of a few per cent in the total amount of energy which we receive would have devastating effects.

The Sun is stable enough at the present time. It is thought that the ice ages which have occurred periodically throughout the Earth's history may be due to small changes in solar output, but these are minor, and a new ice age similar to that of the Pleistocene period would not bring disaster to humanity (though it would certainly introduce complications). However, the Sun

125

will not last for ever, and eventually it must die. Life on the Earth will die with it.

We need have no fears similar to those of the Laputans in Swift's famous novel. Those of us who have read *Gulliver's Travels* will remember how the people of the mythical flying island were haunted by fears that something terrible would happen, 'that the face of the Sun will, by degrees, be encrusted with its own effluvia, and give no more light to the world . . .' and so on. Modern science teaches us that no marked changes are likely for thousands of millions of years. Moreover, the final fate of terrestrial life is likely to be a heat-death, rather than freezing as the Sun fades away.

The source of solar energy is to be found in nuclear processes deep inside the globe. What is happening, basically, is that hydrogen nuclei are combining to form nuclei of helium, releasing energy in the process. The whole problem is a very complex one; it is not fully understood, and certainly cannot be dealt with here. The relevant fact in our present argument is that as the Sun ages, it will become more luminous than it is at present. It may become a 'red giant', and the increased output of radiation will certainly prove fatal to the inner planets at least. Subsequently, it is possible that the Sun will collapse, rather suddenly by cosmical time-standards, into a small, incredibly dense white dwarf, after which it will continue radiating feebly for thousands of millions of years before all its energy leaves it.

If these theories are correct—and we must stress that they cannot be regarded as final—the white dwarf stage will not concern Earthmen, since the preliminary red giant period will have destroyed all life, and possibly our planet as well. But the crisis is so far distant that it is of academic importance only. It will be at least 5000 million years, and probably nearer 10,000 million, before the increase in solar luminosity is enough to make itself felt.

Of course, it is impossible for us to see so far into the future. Whether 'men' will still exist on Earth, we do not know; but if intelligent life survives here by the time that ominous changes occur in the Sun, it is by no means fantastic to suppose that mass migration to another world will take place. Further speculation is clearly pointless.

One other point, however, is worth discussing. Men are new-comers to our world, and have lived here for only a million years or so, whereas the age of the Earth itself is at least 2000 million years, and probably more. If we indulge in a flight of fancy and suppose that explorers from a far-off system had visited Earth in, say, the Pliocene period, they would have found no traces of civilization; 500 million years ago, they would not have found even vegetation—nothing except primitive sea creatures.

This argument may be extended. If we could establish the existence of another habitable planet—moving round Tau Ceti or Epsilon Eridani, for instance—it would need a remarkable coincidence for this planet to harbour intelligent life *at the present epoch*. Life might be still in the primitive stage; it might have appeared, run its evolutionary course and died out; or it might have destroyed itself by internal strife, as *Homo sapiens* is in grave danger of doing today. We have said that our hypothetical visitor would have found no traces of civilization had he arrived here in the Pliocene period. It is only too possible that a visitor in, say, the year A.D. 2000 will find nothing but charred remains upon a highly radioactive Earth.

An analogy may be helpful. Suppose that we have two lamps in a darkened hall, each of which is switched on for ten seconds per day, the periods of luminosity being selected at random. The chances that both lamps will shine simultaneously is extremely small; even so, they are far greater than the chances of two civilizations appearing on neighbouring planets at the same moment. This is yet another reason why the experiments conducted by Drake and his colleagues at Green Bank offer such small hopes of success.

It seems, then, that if we are right in supposing that planetary systems are common in our own and other galaxies, and that life will appear wherever conditions are suitable for it, there must be untold millions of worlds in every conceivable stage of vital development — from primitive marine organisms up to highly intelligent races much more advanced than ourselves. Whether we will ever obtain direct proof is, of course, quite another matter.

We can hope that in the context of the great adventure of

space exploration, the petty jealousies and misunderstandings which divide men will, in a new and truer perspective, be seen to be essentially trivial and time-wasting. There is so much to be discovered, so much to know, and tremendous excitement and pleasure in the process of discovery. A concerted international effort could lead to a rapid advance in our understanding of the Cosmos, and of the nature of living things and their place in the universe. It seems to us that this would be a much healthier mental exercise than the present morbid preoccupation with destruction which afflicts so many of our fellow men.

REFERENCES

CHAPTER I: THE UNIVERSE AROUND US

BRODE, WALLACE R., *Chemical Spectroscopy*. London, 1945.

BROWN, G. I., *An Introduction to Electronic Theories of Organic Chemistry*. London, 1958.

JONES, G. O., ROTBLAT, J., and WHITROW, G. J., *Atoms and the Universe*. London, 1956.

LYTTLETON, R. A., *The Modern Universe*. London, 1957.

MOORE, PATRICK, *Guide to the Stars*. London, 1961.

STRUVE, O., *Elementary Astronomy*. Oxford, 1959.

VAUCOULEURS, G. DE., *Discovery of the Universe*. London, 1956.

CHAPTER II: NATURE AND ORIGIN OF ORGANISMS

[1] CROWTHER, J. G., *Science unfolds the Future*. Chap. VI. Frederick Muller, 1955.

[2] OPARIN, A. I., *The Origin of Life on the Earth*. Oliver and Boyd, London, 1957.

[3] *See* BULLOCH, W., *History of Bacteriology*. London, 1938.

[4] DOBELL, C., *Anthony van Leeuwenhoek and his Little Animals*. Staples Press Ltd., London, 1932.

[5] *See* DE KRUIF, P., *Microbe Hunters*. Jonathan Cape, London, 1936.

[6] TYNDALL, J., *Fragments of Science*, p. 459. Longmans, Green and Co., London, 1876.

[7] *Ibid.*, p. 490.

[8] *See* HARDIN, G., *Sci. Mon.*, **70,** 178. New York, 1950.

[9] BERNAL, J. D., *The Physical Basis of Life*. Routledge and Kegan Paul, London, 1951.

[10] HUXLEY, T. H., *On the Physical Basis of Life*, 1868. Reprinted in *Lectures and Essays*, T. H. Huxley, Thinker's Library, Watts & Co., London, 1931.

[11] VINOGRADOV, A. P., 'The Biological Elements' (in Russian). *Trans. Biogeochemical Lab.*, Nos. 3, 4. Leningrad, Moscow.

[12] *See* FEARON, W. R., *An Introduction to Biochemistry*. London, William Heinemann, Medical Books Ltd., 1949.

[13] BERNAL, J. D., *Science and Industry in the Nineteenth Century*. Routledge & Kegan Paul Ltd., London, 1953.

[14] CRICK, F. H. C., 'The Structure of the Hereditary Material'. In *The Physics and Chemistry of Life*. A Scientific American Book. G. Bell & Sons Ltd., London, 1957.

[15] See *New Biology*, **31**. *Biological Replication*. Penguin Books, 1960.
[16] CALVIN, M., 'Evolution of Enzymes and the Photosynthetic Apparatus'. *Science*, **130**, 1170. 1959.
[17] *See* PERRET, J., *Biochemistry and Bacteria*. *New Biology*, **12**, 69. Penguin Books, 1952.
[18] *See* BERNAL, J. D., 'The Problem of Stages in Biopoesis'. In *The Origin of Life on the Earth*. Pergamon Press, London, 1959.
[19] *See* MASON, B. J., 'Water'. *The New Scientist*, November 14th, 1957, p. 24.
[20] RABINOWITCH, E. I., 'Photosynthesis'. In *The Physics and Chemistry of Life. A Scientific American Book*. G. Bell and Sons Ltd., 1957.
[21] *See* GAFFRON, H., 'Photosynthesis and the Origin of Life'. In *Rhythmic and Synthetic Processes in Growth*. Princeton University Press, 1957.
And see VAN NEIL, C. B., *Advances in Enzymology*, **1**.
[22] EDDINGTON, A. S., *New Pathways in Science*. Cambridge University Press, 1935.
[23] SCHRÖDINGER, E., *What is Life?* Cambridge University Press, 1944.
[24] PIRIE, N. W., 'The Meaninglessness of the Terms Life and Living'. In *Perspectives in Biochemistry*. Cambridge University Press, 1937.
[25] HOROWITZ, N. H., 'On Defining "Life" '. *The Origin of Life on the Earth*, p. 106. Pergamon Press, London, 1957.
[26] PAULING, L., *Ibid.*, p. 119.
[27] PIRIE, N. W., 'On Making and Recognizing Life'. *New Biology*, **16**, 41. Penguin Books, 1954.
[28] SCHÄFER, E. A., *Rep. Brit. Ass.*, p. 3, 1912.
[29] MOORE, B., *Origin and Nature of Life*. Home University of Modern Knowledge, London, Williams & Norgate, 1913.
[30] HALDANE, J. B. S., 'The Origin of Life'. *Rationalist Annual*, 1929. Reprinted in *The Inequality of Man*, by J. B. S. Haldane. Penguin Books, 1937.
[31] NURSALL, J. R., 'Oxygen as a Prerequisite to the Origin of the Metazoa'. *Nature*, **183**, 1170. 1959.
[32] NURSALL, J. R., 'The Origin of the Metazoa'. *Transactions of the Royal Society of Canada*, **LIII**, Series III, June 1959, Section 5, p. 1.
[33] OPARIN, A. I., *Proiskhozhdenie Zhini*. Moscow: Izd. Moskovskii, 1929.
[34] OPARIN, A. I., *The Origin of Life*. Macmillan Co., New York, 1938.
[35] OPARIN, A. I., 'The Origin of Life'. *S.C.R. Soviet Science Bulletin*, III, No. 3, p. 1, 1956.
[36] OPARIN, A. I., 'Introductory Address. First International Symposium.' In *The Origin of Life on the Earth*. Pergamon Press, London, 1959.
[37] OPARIN, A. I., 'Biochemical Processes in the Simplest Structures'. *Ibid.*, p. 428.
[38] DE JONG, B., *see* papers in *Protoplasma*, 1931, 1932.
And see OPARIN, A. I., refs. 2 and 34 above.

REFERENCES

[39] OPARIN, A. I., 'The Problem of the Origin of Life'. *The Modern Quarterly*, **6**, No. 2, 135. 1951.

[40] HALDANE, J. B. S., 'The Origins of Life'. *New Biology*, **16**, 12. Penguin Books, 1954.

[41] MILLER, S. L., 'A Production of Amino-Acids under Possible Primitive Earth Conditions'. *Science*, **117**, 528. 1953.
And see MILLER, S. L., and UREY, H. C., 'Organic Compound Synthesis on the Primitive Earth'. *Science*, **130**, 245. 1959.

[42] MILLER, S. L., *J. Am. Chem. Soc.*, **77**, 2351. 1955.

[43] ABELSON, P. H., 'Amino-acids Formed in "Primitive Atmospheres" '. *Science*, **124**, 935. 1956.

[44] PAVLOVSKAYA, T. E., and PASYNSKII, A. G., 'The Original Formation of Amino-acids under the action of Ultra-Violet Rays and Electrical Discharges'. In *The Origin of Life on the Earth*, p. 151. Pergamon Press, London, 1959.

[45] HASSELSTROM, T., HENRY, M. C., and MURR, B., 'Synthesis of Amino-acids by Beta-Radiation'. *Science*, **125**, 350. 1957.

[46] PASCHKE, R., CHANG, R. W. H., and YOUNG, D., 'Probable Rôle of Gamma-Irradiation in Origin of Life'. *Science*, **125**, 881. 1957.

[47] *See* LIND, S. C., and BARDWELL, D. C., *J. Am. Chem. Soc.*, **48**, 2335. 1926.

[48] SOKOLOV, V., English Abstract:Abstracts of Papers, 17th Int. Geol. Congr., Moscow, 1937.

[49] GARRISON, W. M., MORRISON, D. C., HAMILTON, J. G., BENSON, A. A., and CALVIN, M., 'Reduction of Carbon Dioxide in Aqueous Solutions by Ionizing Radiations'. *Science*, **114**, 416. 1951.

[50] LEDERBERG, J., 'Exobiology: Approaches to Life Beyond the Earth'. *Science*, **132**, 393. 1960.

[51] VINOGRADOV, A. P., 'The Origin of the Biosphere'. In *The Origin of Life on the Earth*, p. 23. Pergamon Press, London, 1959.

[52] GOLDSCHMIDT, V. M., 'Geochemical Aspects of the Origin of Complex Organic Molecules on the Earth, as Precursors to Organic Life'. *New Biology*, **12**, 97. Penguin Books, 1952.

[53] UREY, H. C., 'Primitive Planetary Atmospheres and the Origin of Life'. In *The Origin of Life on the Earth*, p. 16. Pergamon Press, London, 1959.

[54] PIRIE, N. W., 'The Nature and Development of Life and our Ideas about it'. *Modern Quarterly*, **3** (N.S.), 82. 1948.

[55] FOX, S. W., 'A Chemical Theory of Spontaneous Generation'. In *The Origin of Life on the Earth*, p. 257. Pergamon Press, London, 1959.

[56] FOX, S. W., 'Evolution of Protein Molecules and Thermal Synthesis of Biochemical Substances'. *Am. Scientist*, **44**, 347. 1956.

[57] FOX, S. W. *See* report in *The New Scientist*, April 19th, p. 800. 1959.

[58] FOX, S. W., HARADA, K., and KENDRICK, J., 'Production of Spherules from Synthetic Proteinoid and Hot Water'. *Science*, **129**, 1221. 1959.

[59] PRINGLE, J. W. S., 'The Origin of Life', *Symp. Soc. Exptl. Biol.*, **7**, 1. 1953.

[60] PRINGLE, J. W. S., 'The Evolution of Living Matter', *New Biology*, **16**, 54. Penguin Books, 1954.

[61] EYRING, H., and JOHNSON, F. H., 'The Critical Complex Theory of Biogenesis'. In *Influence of Temperature on Biological Systems.* Am. Physiol. Soc., Washington, p. 1. 1957.

[62] KEOSIAN, J., 'On The Origin of Life'. *Science*, **131**, 479. 1960.

CHAPTER III: MYTHS OR MEN?

LEIGHTON, P., *Moon Travellers*. London, 1960.

MOORE, PATRICK., *Science and Fiction*. London, 1957.

NICOLSON, MARJORIE HOPE, *Voyages to the Moon*. London, 1956.

PLUTARCH, *On the Face which appears in the Moon*. Translated by A. O. Prickard. London, 1911.

CHAPTER IV: THE MOON

[1] 'Soviet Moon Rockets.' *Soviet Booklet No. 62*. London, December 1959.

[2] WILKINS, H. P., *Moon Maps*. London, 1960.

[3] KUIPER, G. P. (Editor), *Photographic Lunar Atlas*. London, 1960.

[4] BALDWIN, R. B., *The Face of the Moon*. Chicago, 1949.

[5] MOORE, PATRICK, *Sky and Telescope*, **XV**, 201. 1956. Also *Urania* No. 242. Tarragona, 1956.

[6] MOORE, PATRICK, and CATTERMOLE, P. J., *Journal of the International Lunar Society*, **1**, 16, 70, 103. 1957–9.

[7] KUIPER, G. P., 'The Exploration of the Moon'. *Vistas in Astronautics*, p. 308. London, 1959.

[8] MOORE, PATRICK, 'Problems of the Moon'. *The Advancement of Science*, p. 34. London, May 1960.

[9] MIYAMOTO, S., *Journal of the International Lunar Society*, **I**, 148. 1960.

[10] GOLD, T., 'The Lunar Surface'. *Month. Not. Roy. Astr. Soc.*, **115**, 585. 1955.

[11] PETTIT, E., and NICOLSON, S. B., *Astrophys. Jnl.*, **71**, 102. 1930.

[12] PIDDINGTON, J. H., and MINNETT, H. C., *Aust. J. Sci. Res.*, **2**, 63. 1949.

[13] TROITSKY, B., and ZELINSKAYA, M., *A.J.—U.S.S.R.*, **32**, 550. 1955.

[14] AKABANE, K., *Proc. Japan. Acad.*, **31**, 161. 1955.

[15] GIBSON, J. E., *Proc. Amer. Inst. Rad. Engrs.*, p. 280, January 1958.

[16] JAEGER, J. C., and HARPER, A. F., *Nature*, **166**, 1026. 1950.

[17] MARKOV, A. (Editor), *The Moon*. Moscow, 1960. (In Russian.)

[18] BARABASHOV, N., and CHEKIRDA, A. *On Mountain Rocks bearing a resemblance to those comprising the surface of the Moon*. Kharkov, 1959. (In Russian.)

[19] LIPSKI, Y. N., *Dok. Akad. Nauk.*, **LXV**, 465. 1949.

REFERENCES

[20] KUIPER, G. P., *Proc. Nat. Acad. Sci.*, **40**, 1096. 1954.

[21] COSTAIN, C. H., ELSMORE, B., and WHITFIELD, C. R., *Month. Not. Roy. Astr. Soc.*, **116**, No. 4. 1956.

[22] DOLLFUS, A., 'Nouvelle Recherche d'une Atmosphère du Voisinage de la Lune'. *Comptes Rendus*, **234**. 1952.

[23] FIRSOFF, V. A., *Strange World of the Moon*, p. 129. London, 1959.

[24] PICKERING, W. H., 'Eratosthenes', 1 to 6. *Popular Astronomy*, Nos. 269, 287, 312, 317. 1919-25.

[25] PARKES, A. S., and SMITH, A. U., 'Transport of Life in the Frozen or Dried State'. *Brit. Med. Jnl.*, p. 1295. May 16th, 1959.

[26] SAGAN, C., *Proc. Nat. Acad. Sci. U.S.A.*, **46**, 393.

[27] GILVARRY, J. J., 'Origin and Nature of Lunar Surface Features'. *Nature*, **168**, 886. December 10th, 1960.

CHAPTER V: MARS

[1] DOLLFUS, A., *Comptes Rendus*, **232**, 1066. 1951.

[2] DE VAUCOULEURS, G., *Physics of the Planet Mars*, p. 126. London, 1954.

[3] ANTONIADI, E. M., *La Planète Mars*, p. 44. Paris, 1930.

[4] ÖPIK, E. J., *Irish Astronomical Journal*, **1**, p. 22. 1950.

[5] MOORE, PATRICK, *Guide to Mars*. 2nd edn., London, 1960.

[6] KUIPER, G. P., *Atmospheres of the Earth and Planets*. Chicago, 1949.

[7] DE VAUCOULEURS, G., *op. cit.*, p. 200.

[8] KIESS, C. C., KARRER, S., and KIESS, H. K., 'A New Interpretation of Martian Phenomena'. *Publ. Astr. Soc. Pacific*, **72**, p. 256. 1960.

[9] DOLLFUS, A., *L'Astronomie*, **67**, 103. 1953.

[10] ARRHENIUS, S., *Journal de Physique*, pp. 81-97. 1912.

[11] McLAUGHLIN, D. B., *Publ. Astr. Soc. Pacific*, **66**, p. 161. 1954.

[12] SHARONOV, V. V., *Publ. Leningrad Observatory*, No. 19, p. 202. 1958.

[13] LOWELL, P., *Mars and its Canals*, p. 376. New York, 1906.

[14] DOLLFUS, A., *L'Astronomie*, **67**, p. 96. 1953.

[15] UREY, H. C., 'Primitive Planetary Atmospheres and the Origin of Life'. *Oloe*, p. 16. Moscow.

[16] See *New Biology*, **16**, p. 68: A Note on the Green of Mars.

[17] KUIPER, G. P., *Atmospheres of the Earth and Planets*. Revised edition, Chicago, 1952.

[18] SINTON, W. M., *Astrophys. Jnl.*, **126**, 231. 1957.

[19] SINTON, W. M., 'Further Evidence of Vegetation on Mars'. *Science*, **130**, 1234. 1959.

[20] STRUGHOLD, H., *The Green and Red Planet*. London, 1954.

[21] SMITH, A. U., 'Resuscitation of Frozen Mammals'. *New Scientist*, p. 1153. October 30th, 1958.

[22] PARKES, A. S., 'Biological Effects of Low Temperature'. *New Scientist*, **7**, p. 1057. April 28th, 1960.

[23] NURSALL, J. R., 'Oxygen as a Prerequisite to the Origin of the Metazoa'. *Nature*, **183**, 1170. 1959.

[24] NURSALL, J. R., 'The Origin of the Metazoa'. *Transactions of the Royal Society of Canada*, **LIII,** Series III, Section 5, p. 1. June 1959.

[25] LEDERBERG, J., 'Exobiology: Approaches to Life Beyond the Earth'. *Science,* **132,** 393. 1960.

[26] SPENCER JONES, Sir H., *Life on Other Worlds.* London, 1952.

CHAPTER VI: VENUS

[1] KUIPER, G. P., *Astrophys. Jnl.,* November 1954; *Sky & Tel.,* **XIV,** 131. 1955.

[2] DOLLFUS, A., *L'Astronomie,* **69,** 425. 1955.

[3] MOORE, PATRICK., *The Planet Venus.* 3rd edition, London, 1961.

[4] DOLLFUS, A., *L'Astronomie,* **69,** 418. 1955.

[5] KRAUS, J. D., *Nature,* **178,** 687. 1956.

[6] RICHARDSON, R. S., *Publ. Astr. Soc. Pacific.,* **70,** 251-60. 1958.

[7] OVENDEN, M. W., *Looking at the Stars,* pp. 84, 86. London, 1957.

[8] SINTON, W. M., and STRONG, J., *Science,* **123,** 676. 1956.

[9] KOZYREV, N. A., *Publ. Crimean Astrophys. Obs.,* **12,** 577. 1954.

[10] DUNHAM, P., *Publ. Astr. Soc. Pacific,* **45,** 202. 1932.

[11] ADEL, A., *Astrophys. Jnl.,* **93,** 397. 1941.

[12] WILDT, R., *Astrophys. Jnl.,* **86,** 321. 1937.

[13] WHIPPLE, F. L., and MENZEL, D. H., *Publ. Astr. Soc. Pacific,* **67,** 161. 1955.

[14] LYOT, B., *Ann. Obs. Meudon,* **8,** 7, 66. 1929.

[15] ÖPIK, E. J., *Irish Astronomical Jnl.,* **4,** 37. 1956.

[16] WARNER, B., *Month. Not. Roy. Astr. Soc.,* **121,** 279. 1960.

[17] HOUTGAST, J., *Nature,* **175,** 678. 1955.

[18] KOZYREV, N. A., *Publ. Crimean Astrophys. Obs.,* **12,** 169. 1954.

[19] FIRSOFF, V. A., *Our Neighbour Worlds,* p. 209. London, 1954.

[20] BARABASHOV, N., *Technika Molodezhi,* p. 14. 1960/4.

[21] MAYER, C. H., SLOANAKER, R. M., and McCULLOUGH, T. P., *Sky & Tel.,* **XV,** 435. 1956.

[22] UREY, H. C., *The Planets.* Oxford, 1952.

[23] MOORE, PATRICK, *The Planet Venus.* 2nd edition, London, 1959.

[24] STRUGHOLD, H., *The Green and Red Planet.* London, 1954.

CHAPTER VII: OTHER WORLDS

[1] ANTONIADI, E. M., *La Planète Mercure et la Rotation des Satellites.* Paris, 1934.

[2] PORTER, J. G., 'The Satellites of the Planets'. *J.B.A.A.,* **70,** 33. 1960.

And see WATSON, F. G., *Between the Planets.* Oxford, 1956.

[3] SPENCER JONES, SIR H., *Life on Other Worlds.* Hodder and Stoughton, London, 1959.

REFERENCES

[4] BERNAL, J. D., *The Physical Basis of Life*. Routledge and Kegan Paul, London, 1951.
[5] PEEK, B. M., *The Planet Jupiter*. London, 1959.
[6] HALDANE, J. B. S., 'The Origins of Life'. *New Biology*, **16**, 12. 1954.
[7] LEDERBERG, J., 'Exobiology: Approaches to Life Beyond the Earth'. *Science*, **132**, 393. 1960.
[8] BRIGGS, M. H., 'The Colouring Matter and Radio Emissions of Jupiter'. *The Observatory*, **80**, 159. 1960.

CHAPTER VIII: PLANETS OF OTHER STARS

BONDI, H., *Cosmology*. Cambridge, 1952.
PAYNE-GAPOSCHKIN, C., *Stars in the Making*. London, 1953.
SMART, W. M., *Origin of the Earth*. Cambridge, 1953.
STRUVE, O., *Stellar Evolution*. Princetown University Press, 1950.

CHAPTER X: SUMMARY

[1] LEDERBERG, J., 'Exobiology: Approaches to Life Beyond the Earth'. *Science*, **132**, 393. 1960.

INDEX

577
Jac   3907

Jackson, Francis

AUTHOR   Life in the Universe

TITLE

DATE DUE   BORROWER'S NAME

577
Jac   3907

Jackson, Francis

Life in the Universe

LIFE IN THE UNIVERSE

Books by PATRICK MOORE

The Amateur Astronomer
Earth Satellites (with Irving Geis)
A Guide to the Moon
The Story of Man and the Stars
A Guide to the Stars
How to Make and Use a Telescope (with H. P. Wilkins)
The Planets
Life in the Universe (with Francis Jackson)